4 Titles	5 Salutations	6 Complimentary Close	7 Signature	8 Stationery and Letterheads
14 Quotation Marks	15 Italics	16, 17, 18 Question Mark Exclamation Point Period	19, 20 Parentheses Brackets	21 Capitals
25 Plurals	26 Syllabication	27 Abbreviations	28 Numbers	
32 Sentences	33 Paragraphs	34 Exact Connectives	35 Comparisons	36 Correlatives

40, 41 Conciseness Concreteness	42 Character or Personality	43 Cheerfulness	44 Courtesy	45 Tone

51 Individual Acknowledgments	52 Defective Orders	53 Delayed or Incomplete Shipments	54 Out of Stock	55, 56 Refusals of Orders Remittances
60 Making Credit Inquiries	61 Answering Credit Inquiries	62 Accepting Credit	63 Refusing Credit	64 Business Promotion Letters
68 Structure of Collection Letter	69 Collection Appeals	70 Individual and Form Letters	71, 72 Collection Series Part Payments	73, 74 Extensions Installments
78 Granting Adjustments	79 Refusing Adjustments	80 Other Adjustments	81 Inviting Claims	82 Common Errors
86 Beginnings	87 Desire and Appeals	88 Buying Motives	89 Conviction and Evidence	90 Closes or Clinchers
95 Letters to Business Men	96 Letters to Professional People	97 Letters to Executives	98 Letters to Salesmen	99 Letters to Composite Classes
103 Time Interval	104 Mailing List	105 Tests	106 "Splits"	107 Linking the Letters
111 References and Recommendations	112 Structure: Sales Letter Form	113 Structure: Tabulated Form	114 Structure: Letter and Data Sheet	115 Application Follow-up

Handbook of

BUSINESS CORRESPONDENCE

Handbook of BUSINESS CORRESPONDENCE

John C. McCloskey, Ph.D.
University of Oregon

SECOND EDITION

New York
PRENTICE-HALL, INC.
1951

PRINTED IN THE UNITED STATES OF AMERICA

To

My Mother

Preface

The *Handbook of Business Correspondence* is a compact reference manual designed for the use of businessmen and students. It attempts to present clearly, concisely, and accurately the fundamentals of business correspondence, as reflected by the best writings on the subject and by the letters of firms that make effective use of correspondence in the daily conduct of their business. Its principles are those commonly accepted as standard and given daily practical application in thousands of letters.

In this new edition the contents have been reorganized, many of the articles have been rewritten, new illustrations have been secured, and certain sections, notably those on credit and application letters, have been revised and expanded. A specimen page of envelope addresses is included.

As in the first edition, the charted table of contents makes for easy and quick reference to the materials. Instructors may use it for correctional reference and for inducing the student to acquire a broad acquaintance with the many different situations that confront the business correspondent.

J. C. McCloskey

Acknowledgments

The author wishes to thank the following firms for their helpful suggestions and for permission to make use of their correspondence: American Central Manufacturing Corporation, Underwood Corporation, Remington Rand, Inc., Moore Business Forms, Inc., Wilson H. Lee Company, The National Cash Register Company, The International Nickel Co., Inc., The Bon Marché, Eastman Kodak Company, The American Rolling Mill Co., Ilg Electric Ventilating Co., General Electric Company, Barker Bros., Inc., Studio Girl Shampoo, Hotel Roosevelt, Radio Corporation of America, The B. F. Goodrich Company, National Retail Credit Association, United Air Lines, Railway Express Agency, Charles B. Knox Gelatine Co., Inc., The Penn Mutual Life Insurance Company, Union Pacific Railroad, W. A. Sheaffer Pen Co., United Autographic Register Co., Time, Inc., La Salle Extension University, Frederick and Nelson, Postage and the Mailbag, Fraser-Paterson Co., Lipman Wolfe & Co., Minneapolis-Honeywell Regulator Co., The American Brass Company, Bristol-Myers Company, The International Harvester Company, John Deere Plow Company, Art Metal Construction Company, Standard Accident Insurance Co., Metropolitan Life Insurance Company.

J. C. McCloskey

Contents

CONTENTS

CONTENTS

Handbook of
BUSINESS CORRESPONDENCE

Letter Dress

The Layout

1a. Arrangement and margins.

Arrange the letter attractively on the page. Make the left-hand and right-hand margins not less than one inch wide, and the top and bottom margins a little wider.

Begin the body of the letter two spaces below the salutation, and align it with the margin established by the first line of the inside address.

b. Spacing.

Single space the lines of the letter, and double space between the paragraphs.

c. Form.

In the full block form, the heading, inside address, salutation, lines of the body, complimentary close, signature, reference initials, and enclosure notation all begin at the left margin.

In the modified block form, the lines of the heading begin on the same margin (with letterhead stationery the heading contains only the date line). The lines of the inside address, salutation, and body begin on the margin established by the first line of the inside address. The complimentary close and the signature are blocked and placed on the right-hand side of the page. If the firm name is long, the complimentary close may begin five spaces left of center; no line must extend beyond the right-hand margin. The first line of each paragraph may be indented five or ten spaces.

In the indented form, each succeeding line of the heading and inside address begins five spaces right of the preceding line; the salutation begins at the left margin. The complimentary close may begin five spaces left of center, with the company signature indented five spaces right of the beginning of the complimentary close, or the complimentary close and signature may be blocked and placed on the right side of the page.

In the hanging indention or inverted paragraph form, the heading, inside address, and salutation are blocked. The first line of each paragraph of text begins at the left margin, but the succeeding lines are indented five or ten spaces. The complimentary close and signature are blocked and placed on the right side of the page.

d. Punctuation.

Closed, open, or mixed punctuation may be used with any style of layout.

Closed punctuation places a period after the last line of the heading and the last line of the inside address, the preceding lines being followed by commas; a colon is placed after the salutation, and a comma after the complimentary close.

Open punctuation omits terminal marks at the ends of the lines of the heading, inside address,[1] salutation, and complimentary close.

Mixed punctuation omits terminal marks after the heading and inside address, but places a colon after the salutation and a comma after the complimentary close.

[1] For lines ending with abbreviation, see pp. 71 and 73.

THE LAYOUT

AMERICAN CENTRAL
MANUFACTURING CORPORATION
PRODUCERS OF
American
CONNERSVILLE KITCHENS INDIANA

November 5, 19--

Mrs. Mary F. Sullivan
1774 Alder Street
Eugene, Oregon

Dear Mrs. Sullivan

We are happy to enclose our new "American Kitchens" catalog which you requested.

We sincerely hope that you will be able to use this catalog to good advantage in planning your kitchen.

American Kitchens are the last word in beauty and modern design. We urge that you see the American Kitchen before you remodel or build. Your local American Kitchen dealer is in a position to help you in the development of any plans you may have for your kitchen.

When available, American Kitchen equipment will be well within the limitations of any budget. It will be equally well adapted to the smallest cottage or the manor house. We recommend that you keep in touch with your local American Kitchen dealer or our factory to keep posted on the latest developments in American Kitchens.

Yours very truly

AMERICAN CENTRAL MFG. CORPORATION

W. H. Barlow

W.H.Barlow, Assistant Sales Manager

bmt

Enclosure

Steel Sinks and Cabinets Dishwashers Disposals

Full Block Form with Open Punctuation

[1]

LETTER DRESS

UNDERWOOD CORPORATION

UNDERWOOD, ELLIOTT-FISHER, SUNDSTRAND · SPEED THE WORLD'S BUSINESS

ONE PARK AVENUE

NEW YORK 16, N.Y.

January 16, 19--

Mr. L. T. Brown,
The American Transportation Company,
211 Congress Street,
Boston 12, Massachusetts

Dear Mr. Brown:

We would like to have the opportunity of demonstrating to you how the new Underwood Sundstrand Adding Figuring Machine will save you time and money on figure work in your office, just as it is doing for thousands of other business concerns throughout the world, both large and small, in all lines of business.

The Underwood Sundstrand with its 10-key keyboard and three-point control that promotes high-speed touch operation with the finger tips of ONE HAND is so simple to operate that anyone in your office will be able to add, subtract or multiply figures without bothering to look at the keyboard after only a brief amount of practice.

Will you give our representative but five minutes of your time so that he may demonstrate the Underwood Sundstrand Adding Machine on your own work...in your own office... and at your convenience. There is no obligation. Simply telephone Liberty 7656 and ask for our Regional Manager, Mr. C. H. Prentice. I suggest that you do this today.

Very truly yours,

L. A. Wallinger

Sales Manager
Adding Machine Division

LAW/jcd

Modified Block Form with Closed Punctuation

THE LAYOUT

REMINGTON RAND BUSINESS SERVICE INC.

BUFFALO, N.Y.

November 14, 19--

Mr. Kenneth Fairfield
Johnson Hardware Company
205 E. Sixteenth Street
Chicago, Illinois

Dear Mr. Fairfield:

Thank you for your request for our new book "Let's Take Stock." Your copy is being mailed today.

The Remington Rand visible stock control plan described in this book provides a method whereby you can have, always and instantly in usable form, the facts you need for practical, profitable control of inventories.

Wide usage proves this plan productive of faster turnover, lower investment, and increased profits. Doubling of turnover has not been unusual where this plan has been installed.

The plan has been tested and proved in thousands of organizations under conditions that are never similar. It is "tailor-made"--to meet exactly the conditions and problems in your own business.

A Remington Rand analysis of stock control problems in your office will show you the precise application of the plan that will most effectively increase profits through efficient control of your inventories.

For further information, please write or phone the Remington Rand office at 214 W. Monroe Street.

Yours very truly,

REMINGTON RAND BUSINESS SERVICE INC.

F. J. Hastings

Advertising Department

FJHastings:KD

REMINGTON Typewriters and Accounting Machines — LIBRARY BUREAU Filing Systems and Indexing Service
RAND — KARDEX and INDEX VISIBLE Visible Records — SAFE-CABINET Record Protection Devices
POWERS Tabulating Machines — DALTON Adding and Bookkeeping Machines — KALAMAZOO and BAKER VAWTER Loose Leaf

Modified Block Form with Mixed Punctuation

[1]

INTERTYPE CORPORATION
EXECUTIVE OFFICES • THREE HUNDRED SIXTY FURMAN STREET • BROOKLYN, NEW YORK

NEW YORK, CHICAGO, NEW ORLEANS, SAN FRANCISCO LOS ANGELES AND BOSTON LONDON, BERLIN

November 5, 19--

Mr. Walter A. Post
987 Wilson Street
Emporia, Kansas

Dear Mr. Post:

This letter is written in the form known as the "semi-block" or the "modified block" form.

In this particular letter the paper guide on the typewriter is set so that when the paper is inserted and the marginal stop set at 20, the margin at the left will be two inches wide.

The first line of each paragraph of the body is indented five spaces from the left margin, but each succeeding line begins even with the left margin. To accomplish this, set the marginal stop at 20 and the tabulator stop at 25. The lines of the body are single spaced, with double spacing between the paragraphs.

The first line of the inside address begins at the left margin. The following lines and the salutation begin on the margin established by the first line of the inside address.

Very truly yours,

INTERTYPE CORPORATION

B. W. Jones

B. W. Jones, Manager

BWJ:IB

Modified or Semi-block Form with Mixed Punctuation

THE LAYOUT

MOORE BUSINESS FORMS, Inc.
PACIFIC MANIFOLDING BOOK DIVISION
5750 GREEN ST. • • • EMERYVILLE 8, CALIFORNIA

May 15, 19--

Mr. James F. Black
215 First Avenue
Portland 5, Oregon

Dear Mr. Black:

Accounts are a convenience to both a buyer and a seller. They are based on good business principles and must necessarily be treated by both in a businesslike manner.

At the same time, we try to make every transaction friendly and courteous, even in reminding our friends of their past-due accounts.

May we have your remittance for the amount past due in the same friendly spirit in which we send this letter?

Yours very truly,

MOORE BUSINESS FORMS, INC.

D. C. Edminster

Credit Manager

D.C.Edminster:MS

Indented Form with Mixed Punctuation

[1]

WILSON H. LEE COMPANY
MAILADVERTISING
197 ASYLUM STREET, HARTFORD, CONN.
Telephone 2-9074

October 4, 19--.

Mr. R. A. White,
    324 Oak Street,
        Athens, Ohio.

Dear Mr. White:

This letter is written in the form known as the "indented form," with closed punctuation.

In this particular letter the paper guide on the typewriter is set so that when the paper is inserted and the marginal stop set at 20, the margin at the left will be two inches wide.

The first line of each paragraph of the body is indented five spaces from the left margin, but each succeeding line begins even with the left margin. To accomplish this, set the marginal stop at 20 and the tabulator stop at 25. The lines of the body are single spaced, with double spacing between the paragraphs.

The first line of the inside address begins at the left margin, while each succeeding line begins four spaces to the right of the preceding line.

Very truly yours,

WILSON H. LEE COMPANY

J. L. Knoll

J. L. Knoll, Manager

JLK:RM

Indented Form with Closed Punctuation

THE LAYOUT

THE NATIONAL CASH REGISTER COMPANY
DAYTON, OHIO

August 12, 19--

Western Supply Company, Inc.
910 Market Street
San Francisco 2, California

Attention: Mr. C. F. Johns

Gentlemen:

This letter is written in the form known as the "hanging indention" or "inverted paragraph" form.

In this particular letter the paper guide on the typewriter is set so that when the paper is inserted and the marginal stop set at 20, the left-hand margin of the letter will be two inches wide.

The body of the letter begins two spaces below the salutation. The first line of each paragraph begins at the left margin, and each succeeding line is indented five spaces. To accomplish this, set the tabulator stop at 25. The lines of the body are single spaced, with double spacing between the paragraphs.

The dictator's and the transcriber's initials should be written at the left, a double space below the company signature, or on a line with the department name if one is used. In this letter the firm's name is omitted in the signature, because it appears in the letterhead.

Very truly yours,

James Smith

James Smith
Public Relations

JS:TSW

Enclosure

Hanging Indention or Inverted Paragraph Form with Mixed Punctuation

LETTER DRESS

The Heading

2a. On letterhead stationery, the heading contains only the date, and its position is variable.

The date line may be indented, placed so that its end forms the right-hand margin of the letter, centered below the city and state, begun beneath the first letter in the name of the city, or placed on the same line as the city and state.

GM RADIO

GENERAL MOTORS RADIO CORPORATION

Dayton, Ohio

October 13, 19--

New York Office Hahn Department Stores 1440 Broadway

The Bon Marché

Seattle

November 23, 19—

THE NATIONAL CASH REGISTER COMPANY

DAYTON, OHIO October 15, 19--.

b. When the stationery contains no letterhead (as in an application letter), the address (number and street, city, postal delivery zone number, and state) appears in addition to the date.

THE HEADING

The heading should not be less than one and one-half inches from the top or less than one inch from the right-hand margin. The heading should not extend beyond the right-hand margin.

Block form with open punctuation:

326 Indianola Avenue
Chicago 33, Illinois
July 27, 19—

Indented form with closed punctuation:

19 University Street,
  Seattle 8, Washington,
    August 1, 19—.

c. The postal delivery zone number of the city is placed after the city, and it is followed by a comma.[2]

New York 12, New York

Note: If the city is too small to be zoned, use this form: Eugene, Oregon.

d. Do not place a word or a sign before the street number.

Wrong:

No. 23 Pine Street
Des Moines 8, Iowa
August 26, 19—

#23 Pine Street
Des Moines 8, Iowa
August 26, 19—

Right:

23 Pine Street
Des Moines 8, Iowa
August 26, 19—

[2] For a list of cities using the postal delivery zone number system, see pp. 74-76.

e. **Do not use *d, nd, rd, st,* or *th* following the number of the day.**

Wrong:	April 4th, 19— June 2nd, 19— November 23rd, 19— March 21st, 19—
Right:	April 4, 19— June 2, 19— November 23, 19— March 21, 19—

f. **Do not abbreviate the form of the date.**

Wrong:	6–17–51 6/17/51 6'17'51
Right:	June 17, 1951

g. **Except in rigidly formal writing, do not spell out the day of the month or the year.**

Wrong:	March seventh, Nineteen hundred and fifty-one
Right:	March 7, 1951

h. **Spell out the numeric names of streets and avenues if they are composed of single numbers; express them in figures if they are compounds.**

Right:	Ninth Avenue	73rd Street
	Fifth Street	51st Street
	Tenth Street	132nd Street
	Fortieth Street	East 165 Street

i. **The second page of the letter is a plain sheet without a letterhead but of the same quality and size as the first. It should contain at least two lines of text. Place the heading, containing the name of the addressee, the page number, and the date, two inches from the top of the sheet. Leave four spaces between the heading and the text.**

Examples:

Mr. H. J. White —2— May 15, 19—

or

Prentice-Hall, Inc.
Page 2
February 27, 19—

The Inside Address

3a. The inside address consists of the name of the firm or person to whom the letter is written, the street address, the city, the postal delivery zone number,[3] and the state. The style of the inside address should be consistent with that of the heading.

Block form with open punctuation:

Mr. Andrew F. Parker
4810 Green Street West
Emeryville 7, California

Indented form with closed punctuation:

United Air Lines,
5959 South Cicero Avenue,
Chicago 38, Illinois.

b. Begin the inside address at the left-hand margin of the letter. It should have the same form as the envelope address.

Mr. W. P. Sherwood
456 Pacific Street
Newport, Oregon

Dear Mr. Sherwood:

Here is a little parable that is of more than passing . . .

[3] For a list of cities using the postal delivery zone number system, see pp. 74-76.

[3]

c. **Place the inside address never less than three spaces below the heading, the exact distance depending upon the length of the letter.**

327 First Avenue
Eugene, Oregon
May 8, 19—

Mr. E. T. Brady, President
Apex Novelty Company
Waukegan, Illinois

My dear Mr. Brady:

d. **On the first line type the name of the person or firm addressed. In addressing an individual in a firm, corporation, or other group, write the individual's name on the first line, together with his official title, and the name of the company on the second line.** The business title may, however, be placed on the second line and separated by a comma from the company's name; or if it is long, it may occupy the entire second line. The next line has the street address and the following line the city, postal delivery zone number, and state. If the names of city and state are long, they may be typed on separate lines.

Mr. W. B. Wilbur, Secretary
Zenith Publishing Company
1818 Ronald Street
Cleveland 9, Ohio

Mr. A. F. Logan
Manager, World Publishing Co.
Philomath, Oregon

Mr. H. R. Wilson,
Assistant Advertising Manager,
Hammermill Paper Company,
Erie, Pennsylvania.

Midstates Hardware Company
764 Howell Street
Minneapolis 3
Minnesota

e. In official letters and letters of a personal nature, the inside address may be placed at the lower left-hand corner of the sheet, even with the left margin and two spaces below the typed signature.

Respectfully yours,

George F. Edwards

George F. Edwards

Mr. Roy D. Johnson
980 Nantucket Street
Boston 21, Massachusetts

f. The form of the address should correspond exactly to the official name of the company or firm addressed. If *Co., Company, Inc., The,* or *&* is part of the firm's official name, follow this form in the inside address.

J. K. Dill Company	The First National Bank
Wilson, Hayes & Co.	Blaumauer Drug Co., Inc.

g. Do not abbreviate titles such as *President, Secretary, Treasurer, Manager, Sales Manager,* and *Superintendent.* These titles usually follow the name, which is preceded by *Mr.* (or *Miss* or *Mrs.*).

Mr. John R. Wilde, Treasurer
Willama Knitting Mills
Janesville, Wisconsin

h. Initials indicating degrees, societies, and other honors may follow the name of the person addressed. Use

only the initials of the highest degree. (See p. 72 for a list of abbreviations of academic degrees.)

Wrong: Professor D. V. Tasker, A.B., M.A., Ph.D.
Right: D. V. Tasker, Ph.D.

However, if the degrees are in different fields, they may be used.

Right: Carl Swanson, C.E., LL.D.

i. Never use the word *City* alone in the inside address.

Wrong: Mr. George W. Fielding
23 Main Street
City

Right: Mr. George W. Fielding
23 Main Street
Columbus 3, Ohio

j. Do not place a hyphen or a dash between the house number and the street number.

Wrong: 2120-E. 47th Street
Right: 2120 E. 47th Street

k. Do not use a word or a sign before the street number.

Wrong:
No. 89 Second Street
Oakland 6, California

#89 Second Street
Oakland 6, California

Right:
89 Second Street
Oakland 6, California

l. Spell out the numeric names of streets and avenues if they are composed of single numbers; express them in figures if they are compounds.

Right:

Eighth Avenue	63rd Street
Fourth Street	122nd Street
Sixtieth Street	154 Street

m. To direct the letter to a certain individual in a company, use the *Attention* line after the inside address. With the block form, the *Attention* line begins at the left margin. With the indented form, it is either centered or begun at the paragraph point. The colon is optional. Two spaces should be left above and below the *Attention* line.

United Air Lines
625 S.W. Morrison Street
Portland 5, Oregon

Attention: Mr. John H. Standish

Gentlemen:

General Electric Company,
1 River Road,
Schenectady 5, New York.

Attention of Miss Margaret Erion

Gentlemen:

Railway Express Agency
230 Park Avenue
New York 17, New York

Attention Department of Public Relations

Gentlemen:

Note: The first line of the inside address determines the form of salutation.

n. Type the subject line two spaces below the salutation. It may be centered or begun on the left margin. Arrange long subjects in two lines.

John Whitney & Co., Ltd.
732 Day Street
Seattle 12, Washington

Gentlemen:

Subject: Engineering Estimate

The Jones & Waller Co.
   890 Second Avenue
      Auburn, Nevada

   Attention Mr. F. D. Bosch

Gentlemen:

Subject: Account No. 179A

Titles

4a. In writing the inside address, it is customary to place an appropriate title before the names of individuals.

b. Common titles.

Mr. Used in addressing a man who has no special title or whose title is unknown to the writer.

Mr. James B. Gillespie

Mrs. Used in addressing a married woman. It is customary to address her by her husband's name.

Mrs. Henry F. Shorwell

A widow continues to use her husband's name socially, but in legal and financial matters she is addressed by her own given name.

Mrs. Mary A. Shorwell

A divorced woman usually retains the legal and social right to use her husband's full name.

TITLES

Miss Used in addressing an unmarried woman. Do not use a period after **Miss.** **Misses** is the plural.

Miss Alice Nagle

Misses Alice and Rose Nagle

Messrs. Used in addressing a firm of men, or men and women, when the names denote individuals. Do not use it in addressing corporations or other organizations that bear impersonal names.

Right:

Messrs. Small, Kuhn and Nicoll
Messrs. John Cox & Son
Messrs. Rogers and Watson

Wrong:

Messrs. Illinois Central Railroad
Messrs. American Chemical Company

Right:

Illinois Central Railroad
American Chemical Company

Mesdames (Mmes.) Used in addressing a firm composed of women, whether married or unmarried.

Mesdames Harris and Brown
Mmes. Lange and Lowe

Doctor (Dr.) Used in addressing a man or woman who holds a doctor's degree, as in medicine, theology, law, literature, music, philosophy. Use no other titles with **Dr.**

Wrong:

Dr. Louis B. Woodruff, M.D.

Right:

Dr. Louis B. Woodruff
Louis B. Woodruff, M.D.

Professor (Prof.) Used in addressing university and college teachers of the rank officially designated as *professor*, *associate professor*, or *assistant professor*.

Professor Ralph P. Rollins
Prof. R. P. Rollins

Address other teachers not of the rank of professor, such as college instructors, high-school teachers, teachers in private schools, and teachers in business colleges, as **Mr.** (or **Miss** or **Mrs.**).

Reverend (Rev.) Used in addressing a clergyman.

Reverend (Rev.) William Black
The Reverend William Black
The Reverend Mr. Black (*The first name is omitted with* The Reverend Mr.)

Honorable (Hon.) Used in addressing persons holding high governmental positions, members of municipal and legislative bodies, foreign diplomats, judges, mayors, distinguished lawyers, and, occasionally, prominent citizens. **Hon.** for **Honorable** is conventionally correct.

Honorable Marcus P. Wade
Hon. Paul Le Fevre
Hon. James J. Platt

Rabbi Used in addressing the head of a Jewish house of worship.

Rabbi Stephen H. Bernowitz

Special titles.

POLITICAL OFFICIALS

The President of the United States:

The President
The White House
Washington, D. C.

The President of the United States
The White House
Washington, D. C.

TITLES

The Vice President of the United States:

The Vice President
United States Senate
Washington, D. C.

The Speaker of the House of Representatives:

The Speaker of the House of Representatives
House Office Building
Washington, D. C.

The Honorable Walter A. Hampson
Speaker of the House of Representatives
House Office Building
Washington, D. C.

Cabinet Officers:

The Secretary of State
Washington 25, D. C.

The Honorable Charles R. Swift, Secretary
Department of War
Washington 25, D. C.

The Attorney General of the United States:

The Attorney General of the United States
Washington 25, D. C.

The Honorable William N. Brownson
The Attorney General of the United States
Washington 25, D. C.

Department of Justice
Washington 25, D. C.

Senators:

The Honorable John Archer Colby
Senate Office Building
Washington, D. C.

Senator John Archer Colby
Senate Office Building
Washington, D. C.

[4]

LETTER DRESS

Representatives:

The Honorable John A. Jones
House Office Building
Washington, D. C.

Commissioners:

The Honorable Watson Shirley, Commissioner
United States Office of Education
Washington 25, D. C.

The Chief Justice of the Supreme Court:

The Honorable Henry C. Martin
Chief Justice of the United States
1 First Street N.E.
Washington 13, D. C.

The Chief Justice of the Supreme Court of the United States
1 First Street N.E.
Washington 13, D. C.

Associate Justices of the Supreme Court

The Honorable Henry V. Dahlberg
Associate Justice of the Supreme Court of the United States
1 First Street N.E.
Washington 13, D. C.

District Judges:

The Honorable Lawrence T. Campbell
Lane District Court
Lane, Ohio

Governors:

The Honorable Oliver P. Shiras
Governor of Iowa
Des Moines 10, Iowa

The Honorable Horace X. Jones
Executive Mansion
Albany, New York

The Honorable
The Governor of Idaho
Boise, Idaho

Lieutenant Governors:

The Honorable Ben J. Reilley
Lieutenant Governor of Washington
Olympia, Washington

State Senators and Assemblymen:

The Honorable Gordon E. Lovell
The State Senate
Des Moines 10, Iowa

Senator Myron K. Whipple
The State Capitol
Olympia, Washington

The Honorable Percival G. Kress
Member of the Assembly
Albany, New York

Assemblyman Walter C. Overton
Assembly Chamber
The State Capitol
Harrisburg, Pennsylvania

Mayors:

The Honorable Harold S. Channing
Mayor of the City of San Francisco
City Hall
San Francisco 1, California

The Mayor of the City of San Francisco
City Hall
San Francisco 1, California

American Ambassador:

The Honorable
Jefferson Caffrey
American Ambassador
Paris, France

Foreign Ambassador:

His Excellency
The Ambassador of France
2129 Wyoming Avenue N.W.
Washington 8, D. C.

UNIVERSITY AND COLLEGE OFFICIALS

President of a University or College:

Dr. Harry K. Newburn, President
University of Oregon
Eugene, Oregon

President Harry K. Newburn
University of Oregon
Eugene, Oregon

Harry K. Newburn, Ph.D.
President, University of Oregon
Eugene, Oregon

Dean of a University or College:

Dr. Frederick M. Thompson
Dean of the College of Liberal Arts
University of Wisconsin
Madison 3, Wisconsin

Dean Frederick M. Thompson
College of Liberal Arts
University of Wisconsin
Madison 3, Wisconsin

Mrs. Fanny McGuire
Dean of Women
Oregon State College
Corvallis, Oregon

University or College Professors:

Professor Frank S. Reed
Department of Physics
University of Colorado
Boulder, Colorado

Dr. Stanley R. Phillips
Department of English
University of Minnesota
Minneapolis 17, Minnesota

Stanley O. Ward, Ph.D.
Professor of Latin
Tulane University
New Orleans 11, Louisiana

Note: Dr., Ph.D., and similar abbreviations may be used only if the person addressed possesses the degree so indicated; if in doubt, consult the faculty roster in the catalogue of the institution addressed.

University or College Instructors:

Dr. William W. Mitchell
School of Business Administration
University of Oregon
Eugene, Oregon

Mr. Herbert D. Abernathy
Department of Romance Languages
Lawrence College
Appleton, Wisconsin

Note: See note on "University or College Professors." If an instructor does not possess a Ph.D. or an honorary doctoral degree, he must be addressed as *Mr.*, or *Mrs.*, or *Miss.* An instructor cannot be addressed as *Professor*; he must be addressed as *Mr.*, or, if appropriate, as *Dr.*

THE ROMAN CATHOLIC HIERARCHY

The Pope:

His Holiness, Pope Pius XII
Vatican City

His Holiness, the Pope
Vatican City

Cardinals:

His Eminence, John Cardinal Moore

If also an archbishop:
His Eminence, The Cardinal Archbishop of Denver

[4]

LETTER DRESS

His Eminence, John Cardinal Moore
Archbishop of Denver

Archbishops:

His Grace, the Archbishop of Dubuque

The Most Reverend Archbishop of Dubuque

The Most Reverend Edward D. Howard, D.D.
Archbishop of Portland in Oregon

Bishops:

The Most Reverend Thomas J. Quinn
Bishop of Oregon City

Monsignors:

Right Reverend Monsignor John J. Hurley

President of a College, Religious Supervisor, or Dean:

Very Reverend John T. Kelly (the abbreviation of the order or community follows the name and is set off from it by a comma; no abbreviation follows the names of secular priests).

Abbots:

Right Reverend Abbot Bernard, O.S.F.

Monks:

Reverend Father Francis, O.S.B.

Priests:

Reverend (or Rev.) Michael J. Flynn (secular priest)

Reverend (or Rev.) John J. Schulte, S.J. (if a member of a religious community or order)

College President:

The Very Reverend Thomas Plassman, O.F.M.
President, St. Bonaventure College
St. Bonaventure, New York

TITLES

Members of a Brotherhood:

Brother Paul, O.S.F.

Brother Bernard T. Tobin, S.M.

Members of a Sisterhood:

Sister Mary Doloroso, B.V.M.

Superior of a Sisterhood:

Mother Mary Lydia, O.S.F.

Reverend Mother Mary Lydia, O.S.F.

Reverend Mother Superior, B.V.M.

THE PROTESTANT CLERGY

Episcopalian Bishops:

The Right Reverend William A. Rhodes
Bishop of the Episcopal Diocese
Seattle 5, Washington

Deans:

Dean Lawson F. Whittlesey

The Very Reverend Dean Lawson F. Whittlesey

Methodist Bishops:

Reverend Bishop George A. Martin

Other Clergymen:

The Reverend John T. Adams

Rev. John T. Adams

Rev. Dr. J. T. Adams

The Rev. J. T. Adams, D.D.

THE JEWISH FAITH

Rabbi Stephen Weinberg

Reverend Stephen Weinberg

LETTER DRESS

Salutations

5a. Type the salutation on a separate line two spaces below the inside address and even with the left margin.

Mr. C. H. Whitney, Sales Manager
Peosta Hardware Company
Dubuque, Iowa

Dear Mr. Whitney:

b. Use a colon after the salutation if the punctuation of the heading and inside address is closed or mixed; if it is open, omit the colon.

My dear Mr. Allen:

Gentlemen

c. Always capitalize the first word of the salutation. Capitalize *dear* only when it is the first word of the salutation.

Dear Sir:
My dear Sir:
Madam:
My dear Miss West:

d. Common salutations.

(1) Very formal.

My dear Sir:
Sir:
My dear Madam:
Madam:

(2) Formal.

Dear Sir:
Dear Madam: (*used in addressing a married woman or an unmarried woman*)

Gentlemen: (*used in addressing two or more men, a company, firm, corporation, post office box number, committee, or a firm composed of both men and women*)
Mesdames: (*used in addressing two or more women or a firm composed of women*)

(3) Less formal and implying personal acquaintance or previous correspondence. The tendency is to use the more personal forms, as *Dear Mr. White* instead of *Dear Sir*.

Dear Mr. White:
My dear Mr. White:
Dear Mrs. White:
My dear Mrs. White:
Dear Miss White:
My dear Miss White:

(4) Informal forms used only in writing to one's personal friends.

Dear White:
My dear White:
Dear John:

(5) Official letter salutations.

Sir:
Sirs:
Gentlemen:

e. *Dear Sirs* is still used by conservative institutions, banks, and lawyers.

f. Never use *Messrs.* and *Miss* as salutations.

Wrong:
Messrs. Kandle and Kane:
Dear Miss:

Right:
Gentlemen:
Dear Madam:

g. Do not abbreviate titles in salutations except *Mr., Mrs.,* and *Dr.*

Wrong:	*Right:*
D'r. Sir:	Dear Sir:
Dear S'r.:	Dear Sir:
Gents.:	Gentlemen:
Mmes.:	Mesdames:

h. Do not use a person's name alone as a salutation.

Wrong: Mr. Wallace Mooney:
Right: My dear Mr. Mooney:

i. If the first line of the inside address bears the name of a company, firm, corporation, or partnership, make the salutation plural. If the first line of the inside address bears the name of an individual, make the salutation singular.

Underwood Corporation
1 Park Avenue
New York 16, New York

Gentlemen:

Mr. L. H. Taylor, Sales Manager
The B. F. Goodrich Company
Akron 3, Ohio

Dear Mr. Taylor:

Hotel Roosevelt
Madison Avenue and 45th Street
New York 17, New York

Attention Mr. Dean Carpenter, General Manager

Gentlemen:

(*Note:* The *Attention* line does not affect the salutation.)

j. Special salutations.

SALUTATIONS

POLITICAL OFFICIALS

The President of the United States:

The President: (very formal; official)
Mr. President: (formal)
My dear Mr. President: (informal)

The Vice President of the United States:

Sir: (formal)
My dear Mr. Vice President: (informal)

The Speaker of the House of Representatives:

Sir: (formal)
My dear Mr. Speaker: (informal)

Cabinet Officers:

Sir: *or* Dear Sir: *or* My dear Sir:
My dear Mr. Secretary:
My dear Mr. Stewart:

The Attorney General of the United States:

Sir: *or* Dear Sir: *or* My dear Sir:
My dear Mr. Attorney General:

Senators:

Sir: *or* Dear Sir: *or* My dear Sir:
My dear Senator:
My dear Senator Colby:

Representatives:

Sir: *or* Dear Sir: *or* My dear Sir: *or* My dear Madam:
My dear Congressman:
My dear Mr. Jones:
My dear Madam Smith:
My dear Congresswoman:

Commissioners:

Sir: *or* Dear Sir: *or* My dear Sir:
My dear Mr. Shirley:

[5]

LETTER DRESS

The Chief Justice of the Supreme Court:

Sir: *or* Dear Sir: *or* My dear Sir:
My dear Mr. Chief Justice:
My dear Mr. Martin:

Associate Justices of the Supreme Court:

Sir: *or* Dear Sir: *or* My dear Sir:
My dear Mr. Justice:
My dear Mr. Dahlberg:

District Judge:

Sir: *or* Dear Sir: *or* My dear Sir:
My dear Judge Campbell:

Governors:

Sir: *or* Dear Sir: *or* My dear Sir:
Your Excellency:
My dear Governor Shiras:

Lieutenant Governors:

Sir: *or* Dear Sir: *or* My dear Sir:
My dear Lieutenant Governor:

State Senators and Assemblymen:

Sir: *or* Dear Sir: *or* My dear Sir:
Dear Senator Lovell:
Dear Mr. Whipple:
My dear Representative Kress:

Mayors:

Sir: *or* Dear Sir: *or* My dear Sir:
My dear Mr. Mayor:
My dear Mayor Channing:

Ambassadors:

Sir: (formal)
My dear Mr. Ambassador: (informal)

SALUTATIONS

UNIVERSITY AND COLLEGE OFFICIALS

President of a University or College:

Dear Sir: *or* My dear Sir:
Dear Dr. Taylor:
Dear President Taylor:

Dean of a University or College:

Dear Sir: *or* My dear Sir:
Dear Dr. Thompson:
My dear Dean Thompson:
Dear Mrs. McGuire: (*or* Dear Dr. McGuire: if entitled to "Dr.")

University or College Professors:

Dear Sir: *or* My dear Sir:
Dear Professor Reed:
Dear Dr. Phillips:
Dear Mr. Bailey: (if not entitled to "Dr.")

University or College Instructors:

Dear Sir: *or* My dear Sir:
Dear Dr. Mitchell: (if entitled to "Dr.")
Dear Mr. Abernathy: (if not entitled to "Dr.")
Dear Mrs. (*or* Miss) White: (or Dr. if entitled to "Dr.")

THE ROMAN CATHOLIC HIERARCHY

The Pope:

Your Holiness:
Most Holy Father:

Cardinals:

Your Eminence:

Archbishops:

Your Excellency:
Your Grace:
Most Reverend Archbishop:

[5]

LETTER DRESS

Bishops:

Your Excellency:
Most Reverend and dear Bishop:
My dear Bishop:

Monsignors:

Right Reverend and dear Monsignor:
Dear Monsignor Blank:

President of a College, Religious Supervisor, or Dean:

Very Reverend and dear Father:

Abbots:

Right Reverend and dear Abbot Blank:

Monks:

Reverend Father:
Reverend dear Father:
Dear Father Francis:

Priests:

Reverend Father:
Reverend dear Father:
Dear Father Flynn:

Members of a Brotherhood:

Dear Brother:
Dear Brother Paul:

Members of a Sisterhood:

Dear Sister:
My dear Sister:
Dear Sister Therese:
My dear Sister Mary Doloroso:

Superior of a Sisterhood:

Reverend Mother:
My dear Reverend Mother:
Reverend Mother Mary Lydia:

Dear Mother General:
Dear Mother Superior:
Dear Sister Superior:

THE PROTESTANT CLERGY

Episcopalian Bishops:

Right Reverend and dear Sir:
My dear Bishop Rhodes:

Deans:

Very Reverend Sir:
My dear Dean Whittlesey:

Methodist Bishops:

Dear Bishop Martin:
My dear Bishop Martin:
Dear Sir:

Other Clergymen:

Dear Sir: *or* My dear Sir:
Reverend Sir:
Dear Dr. Adams: (if entitled to "Dr.")
Dear Mr. Adams:

THE JEWISH FAITH

Dear Sir: *or* My dear Sir:
Reverend Sir:
My dear Rabbi Weinberg:
Dear Dr. Weinberg: (if entitled to "Dr.")
My dear Mr. Weinberg:

The Complimentary Close

6a. Place the complimentary close on a separate line two spaces below the last line of the body of the letter. With the full block style, type it at the left margin.

This is the last line of the body of the letter.

Very truly yours

With the modified block and indented styles, type it five spaces to the left of center, or at the center, or a

little to the right of center. The complimentary close never extends beyond the right-hand margin.

This is the last line of the body of the letter.
Very truly yours,

This is the last line of the body of the letter.
Very truly yours,

b. Capitalize only the first word of the complimentary close.

Yours very truly,

Very truly yours,

Yours truly,

c. If the punctuation is either closed or mixed, place a comma after the complimentary close.

Very truly yours,

If the punctuation is open, omit the comma.

Very truly yours

d. Forms of the complimentary close.

(1) Common closes.

Yours truly,
Yours very truly,
Very truly yours,

(2) Personal and friendly closes. (The use of these closes is governed by the relations of the writer and the reader; they are used only when they agree with the salutation in familiarity and tone.)

Sincerely,
Yours sincerely,
Sincerely yours,
Most sincerely,
Very sincerely,
Cordially,
Cordially yours,
Yours cordially,

(3) **Formal closes.** (Use these closes in addressing superiors in rank and high officials in business, or to show deep or special respect.)

Respectfully,
Yours respectfully,
Respectfully yours,
Very respectfully yours,

(4) **Official letter closes.** (Use these closes in addressing high governmental officials.)

Respectfully,
Yours respectfully,
Yours truly,
Yours very truly,
Very truly yours,

Note: Yours truly is always correct. *Yours very truly* and *Very truly yours* are the most popular closes. Use *Respectfully* only to show deep respect. Use *Cordially* when friendship exists between you and the reader and when the letter itself is warm and cordial.

e. Do not use the following closes:

and oblige,
I am,
Believe me,
I beg to remain,
Yours for bigger business,
Yours for better business,
Yours for more business,
Yours for a bigger year,
Yours for a big year,
Yours for prosperity,
Yours until Niagara Falls,
(or any other "smart" or "clever" close)
Hoping, thanking, *or any other participial closes*
Y'rs., Resp'y., *or any other abbreviations*

f. Make the complimentary close agree with the salutation in tone and degree of formality or familiarity.

Salutations	*Corresponding Closes*
Dear Sir:	Yours truly,
or	Yours very truly,
Dear Madam:	Very truly yours,
My dear Sir:	Yours truly,
or	Yours very truly,
My dear Madam:	Very truly yours,
Gentlemen:	Yours very truly,
or	Very truly yours,
Mesdames:	Yours truly,
Dear Mr. Lane:	Yours very truly,
or	Very truly yours,
Dear Mrs. Lane:	Sincerely yours,
or	Very sincerely yours,
Dear Miss Lane:	Yours very sincerely,
	Yours most sincerely,
Sir:	Respectfully yours,
	Very respectfully yours,
Dear Ted:	Cordially,

The Signature

7a. Place the signature two spaces below the complimentary close, on the same margin (block) or five spaces to the right (indented). Do not have it extend beyond the right-hand margin.

Yours very truly,

MILWAUKEE SUPPLY CO.

Ronald Meany

Ronald Meany
Advertising Department

Yours very truly,

WHITESIDE BROTHERS

W. F. Vincent

W. F. Vincent
Credit Manager

b. Should the signature consist only of the name of the writer (as in the Application letter), type it four spaces below the complimentary close, and place the handwritten signature between the complimentary close and the typed signature.

Yours very truly,

E. F. Harrison

E. F. Harrison

c. It is not necessary to place *per* or *by* before the signature, nor is it necessary to indicate the place for the signature by a dotted line.

d. In letters from firms, type the firm name two spaces below the complimentary close. Type the writer's name four spaces below the firm name, and his title, position, or department on the same line or on the next line. Place the handwritten signature between the firm name and the typed signature.

Yours very truly,

THE AMERICAN CAN COMPANY

George F. Edwards

George F. Edwards, President

[7]

LETTER DRESS

Very truly yours,

NORTHERN LIFE COMPANY

Paul T. Bates

Paul T. Bates
Adjustment Department

Very truly yours,

ROSSWIN PHARMACAL CO.

T. A. Smith

T. A. Smith/MR Secretary

Note: Because of the difference in length of signatures, firm names, titles, and the names of official positions and departments, the form of the signature varies. Consequently, experience is necessary to secure the most pleasing arrangement.

Very truly yours,

COMMITTEE ON RECOMMENDATION
OF TEACHERS

Frances M. Camp

Frances M. Camp
FMC:MSH Director

e. In many firms, it is the policy with letterhead stationery to omit the company name in the signature.

Very truly yours,

Norman J. Kelly
Sales Manager

f. **When the name of the dictator and his official title are given in the letterhead, the official title is sometimes omitted in the signature.**

Yours very truly,
SALEM BOX COMPANY

Seneca Smith

g. **An unmarried woman signs her full name preceded by *Miss* in parentheses. However, *Miss* often is omitted, since it is taken for granted that the woman is unmarried if *Mrs.* does not appear before her name.**

Very truly yours,

(Miss) Joan Randall

Yours very truly,

Rosemary Crashaw

h. A married woman signs her own name preceded by *Mrs.* in parentheses, or with her married name in parentheses below her signature.

Very truly yours,

Mary E. Foster

(Mrs.) Mary E. Foster

Very truly yours,

Alice B. Wortham

Alice B. Wortham
(Mrs. John H. Wortham)

i. A widow continues to use the full given name of her husband socially (Mrs. John Archer), but in legal and financial matters, she signs her own given name in the same manner as a married woman (Mrs. Helen Archer).

Yours very truly,

Emma S. Wood

(Mrs.) Emma S. Wood

j. A divorcee socially uses her husband's full name (Mrs. James F. Hill), but if she prefers she may use her maiden surname and her husband's surname (Mrs. Sue Scott Hill), unless she legally resumes her maiden name. In legal and financial matters, she signs in the same manner as a married woman

(Mrs. Sue S. Hill), unless her name has legally been changed.

k. Ordinarily, business women need not use *Miss* or *Mrs.* when signing letters for the company with which they are connected.

l. No titles except *Mrs.* and *Miss* ever precede the signature. Such degrees as M.A., M.D., and LL.D. never follow the signature. The writer's address should not be included with the signature.

m. Do not use a rubber stamp signature. Write the signature legibly with pen and ink and avoid crowding it to the bottom of the page. Do not use variant signatures. Such phrases as "dictated but not read" are never permissible.

n. Place the reference initials, that is, the initials of the dictator (signature identification) and those of the stenographer (stenographic reference), flush with the left margin and two spaces below the last line of the signature. Always place the initials of the dictator first, and separate them from those of the stenographer by a colon or some other mark of punctuation.

GFE:DS

JMC-F

T. A. Smith/IMR

JCConway
PB

Note: When the dictator's name is typed in the signature, his initials may be omitted from the reference notation.

o. Place a reference to enclosures flush with the left margin and one or two spaces below the reference initials.

CJM:RL
Enclosure

HTS/IPB
Encl.

JCC:ML
2 encls.

OSF:H
Encl. 3

JLK:KC
Enclosures:2

EDV/UP
One enclosure

Stationery and Letterheads

8a. **The stationery should be of good quality, usually white, and of standard size, 8½ by 11 inches, so as to fit the standard envelope, 6½ by 3½ inches. Ordinarily, black ribbon is used.**

b. **Letterheads should be simple, distinctive, and dignified. They should be attractively designed to indicate the character of the house, and should not occupy more than one-fifth of the sheet.**

c. **Letterheads should contain only necessary information, such as the name and address of the firm, the kind of business, and the telephone number. Sometimes, however, they include the cable address, the trade-mark, the names of a few officers, the name of a branch office, or the name of a department.**

d. **It is not advisable to distract the reader's attention from the message by pictures, elaborate trade-marks, long lists of officers, or advertising matter extending down the margins.**

e. These are examples of effective letterheads:

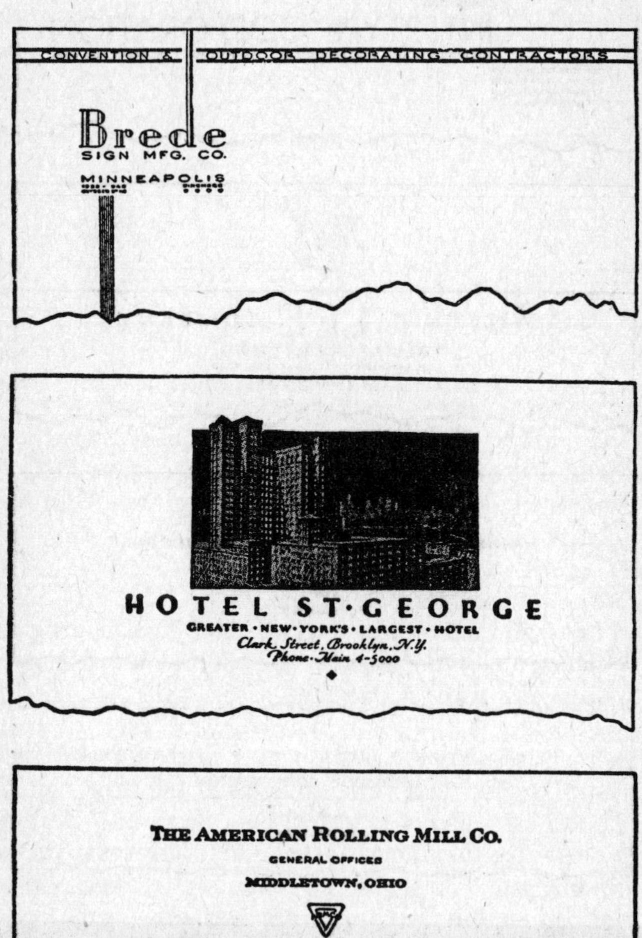

[8]

LETTER DRESS

INTERTYPE CORPORATION

EXECUTIVE OFFICES • THREE HUNDRED SIXTY FURMAN STREET • BROOKLYN, NEW YORK

NEW YORK, CHICAGO, NEW ORLEANS, SAN FRANCISCO LOS ANGELES AND BOSTON LONDON, BERLIN

the WILSON H. LEE COMPANY

MAILADVERTISING

107 ASYLUM STREET, HARTFORD, CONN

Telephone 2-9074

REMINGTON RAND BUSINESS SERVICE INC.

BUFFALO, N.Y.

UNDERWOOD CORPORATION

UNDERWOOD, ELLIOTT-FISHER, SUNDSTRAND • SPEED THE WORLD'S BUSINESS

ONE PARK AVENUE

NEW YORK 16, N.Y.

UNITED AIR LINES

Punctuation and Capitals

The Comma

9a. Use a comma to separate independent clauses joined by *and, but, for, or, nor, yet.*

Each act is a display of skating skill and theatrical art, and each performer is a star in his own right.

The past-due amount is not large, but frequently small amounts that have become delinquent create the wrong impression of your credit standing.

You can whip up piles of thick, luscious cream in two minutes, for all you have to do is flip a switch.

b. Separate by commas the members of a series of coordinate words, phrases, or clauses.

Allura Facial Cream removes stubborn make-up safely, gently, thoroughly and leaves your skin soft, satiny, and dewy-moist.

Would you like to have someone plan your next year's crop, tell you how to protect your soil, and pay you for it?

Picture the flash of steel on a circle of shimmering ice, a chorus of fifty whose every movement spells grace, rhythm, and perfect coördination, and an array of breath-taking costumes.

Please inform us specifically where you were educated, what experience you have had, and whether you have any preference for factory or field work.

c. An introductory dependent phrase or clause is usually separated from the main clause by a comma.

Knowing that you make it a point to be prompt in your payments, we are sure that you will send us a remittance upon receipt of this reminder.

For your convenience, a financial statement blank is enclosed.

If there is any delay, notify us by wire.

As you are driving along the highway alone at night, a Zenith installed in your car will bring you friendly company.

d. Set off by commas non-restrictive modifiers—either phrases or clauses. Do *not* set off restrictive modifiers.

Non-restrictive:

You are invited to our annual party, which is to be held in the gaily decorated ballroom of the Oceanview Hotel.

We ask that you fill out and return the blank to our store, giving us the information needed for our credit files.

Restrictive:

Congratulations on the opening of your new store in our city.

A blow-out results in a car that is crazily out of control.

It is our organization's policy to ask for certain information when a new customer seeks to establish a credit account with us.

Accounts that become delinquent create an unfavorable impression of your credit standing.

e. Wherever necessary, use a comma to prevent misunderstanding.

Inside, every bit of the ham is tender.

When you telephone, your nearest grocer will deliver promptly.

f. With closed or mixed punctuation, place a comma after the last word of the complimentary close.

Very truly yours,

With open punctuation, omit the comma.

Very truly yours

g. Set off by commas the words that introduce a direct quotation.

The manager said, "All our salesmen have remarkable records."

"All our salesmen," said the manager, "have remarkable records."

Note: Commas and periods are placed *inside* the quotation marks.

h. Set off words of direct address.

Donald, I have a plan which will pay you extra money for your spare hours.

Steaming hot water, Mr. Willoughby, is instantly available.

i. Set off parenthetical expressions.

The Glenco is our best auto radio and will, we are sure, give you lasting satisfaction.

This request is, of course, one of the customary formalities in opening a new account.

j. Set off the nominative absolute.

Your feeling about the matter being what it is, we are very glad you took the opportunity to write us.

The job done, the mechanic departed.

k. Set off interjections expressing mild emotion.

Oh, did you buy one too?

l. Set off *yes, no, surely, well, indeed, perhaps, for example, certainly, possibly, accordingly, now,* and similar introductory words modifying the entire predication.

At a shipyard in North Carolina, for example, six of these locomotives are handling heavy switching easily and economically.

You will agree, surely, that we have been patient in requesting payment of this long-due account.

Yes, it's easy to select pieces that fit your budget.

Also, its long-wearing qualities make it ideally suited to business floors.

m. Set off *then, therefore,* and similar emphatic or summarizing adverbs.

It is difficult, therefore, to understand your failure to respond to our request for payment of your delinquent account.

n. Set off an appositive, except when the appositive is considered a part of the name or when some other distinguishing mark of punctuation is used to set it off from the name.

Our representative, Mr. Charles Singer, will assist you in planning an effective window display.

Vegetables, such as tomatoes and spinach, are healthful.

But: My son Peter, St. John the Divine, The book *Modern Business Methods,* the poem "Lycidas"

o. Set off titles following proper names.

Charles Lawrence, Ph.D., teaches history.

Geoffrey Connor, M.P., will visit Canada.

Roland Richards, Secretary of the Treasury, spoke at Trenton.

p. Set off the year from the day of the month, the city from the street address or office building, and the state from the city. If a postal delivery zone number is necessary, it is placed after the city and is separated from the state by a comma.

On September 9, 1947, our firm was organized.

Send your application to our home office at 3349 Fairmount Avenue, Detroit 17, Michigan.

Our representative in your territory is Mr. George Tucker, 301 Southland Life Building, Dallas 1, Texas.

q. It is customary to omit the comma before the *and* in the name of a business firm.

Benson, Hedges and Waldorf; Ackerman, Glover & Clay

r. Separate *Inc.* or *Ltd.* from the firm's name.

Consolidated Chemicals, Inc.
Redwine, Johnson, Ltd.

The Semicolon

10a. Use a semicolon between independent clauses not joined by a coördinating conjunction (*and, but, for, or, nor, yet*).

The flour works with any recipe you have; it largely eliminates failure in cake making.

Before an applicant receives a position, the employer wants to know certain facts; for example, he wants to know about the training and experience of the applicant.

Oil should be changed regularly; that is, the crankcase should be drained every thousand miles.

b. Use a semicolon between independent clauses joined by a conjunctive adverb (*therefore, so, moreover, hence, still, accordingly, nevertheless, furthermore, consequently, also, otherwise, however, likewise, thus, then, besides*).

Your account must be paid in full by the tenth; otherwise we shall have to turn it over to a collection agency.

Eversharp's dual ink reservoir furnishes an emergency supply of ink whenever the main well runs dry; hence the writer is always warned in plenty of time to refill his pen.

c. When the clauses of a compound sentence contain interior punctuation or when they have a complicated

structure, the semicolon may be used for clearness, even though the clauses are joined by a coördinating conjunction.

Keep Goodrich in mind when you need new tires, tubes, or batteries; recapping and repair service; or other needs, such as fan belts, radiator hose, flares, light bulbs, and fuses.

d. To use a comma or no punctuation at all in place of the semicolon is to commit the comma fault.

Comma fault: We liked the car, therefore we bought it.
We liked the car therefore we bought it.

Right: We liked the car; therefore we bought it.

The Colon

11a. The colon is a formal mark of introduction to a list, a statement, a question, a long quotation, a series of statements or questions, a series of examples, a formal appositive, or a word.

The boxes come in four colors: blue, white, yellow, and green.

Our clients say there are only two reasons: a college education or a better than average start in life.

The question before the council is this: How can our men be given work?

The speaker continued: "When it becomes evident that the progress of the country is materially advanced by the invention of labor-saving devices which permit the worker to benefit himself by the intelligent employment of his leisure time, then it becomes a national duty to encourage these inventions and their inventors."

On the reverse side of the chart is another of the basic Knox recipes: Spanish Cream.

b. Use a colon to separate the following: an act of a play from a scene, the title of a book from its subtitle, a

publisher's name from the place of publication, and a chapter of the Bible from a verse.

Merchant of Venice, I:2, 20–30.

The Wealth of the American People: A History of Their Economic Life. New York: Prentice-Hall, Inc., 1949.

Luke II:9–14.

c. With closed or mixed punctuation, place a colon after the salutation of a letter.

Gentlemen:
Dear Sir:
My dear Miss Layden:

With open punctuation, omit the colon.

Dear Mr. Smith

d. Use a colon to separate the hour of the day from the minutes.

4:15 A.M.
10:37 P.M.

The Dash

12a. Use the dash to indicate a sudden shift in the thought of the sentence, an abrupt change of construction, uncertainty on the speaker's part, an afterthought, or emphasis.

Won't you save us the expense and embarrassment of again asking—but surely the matter has simply slipped your mind.

The enclosed pamphlet pictures the most popular model in our line of diesel-electric locomotives—the 45-tonner.

We want you to buy early—before December 1.

b. The dash may be used informally in place of the parentheses or the comma.

We want you to read the next three issues of the *Journal of Living*—without risking a penny—and see for yourself how it can help you to better health.

When a man is puzzled over the dozens of problems that come up in everyday business—buying, selling, advertising, and managing a store—little matters like the enclosed account easily slip out of mind.

c. The dash may be used to mark off a statement summarizing preceding matter.

This construction principle gives far greater bruise resistance and longer wear—features especially desirable on heavy-load, rough-going service.

If you want to visit our showrooms, if you want to inspect and investigate, if you want to make real comparisons—if you want to do these things before you buy, we invite you to visit us.

The Apostrophe

13a. Use an apostrophe to indicate the omission of letters or figures.

can't, don't, won't, doesn't

b. Use *'s* to form the plural of letters, words, numbers, and signs.

Besides too many *g's*, the sentence contained three *and's*, four *9's*, and two *&'s*.

c. Add *'s* to form the possessive of a noun, singular or plural, not ending in *s*.

company's, boy's, horse's, father's, men's, children's

d. To form the possessive of plural nouns that end in *s*, add only the apostrophe.

boys' games; sophomores' record; actors' salaries; soldiers' courage; cows' milk

e. To form the possessive of proper nouns ending in *s*, add *'s* to nouns of one syllable, and only the apostrophe to words of more than one syllable.

Keats's poems; Burns's works; Dickens' novels

f. In firm names add *'s* or only the apostrophe to the last word in the firm name to indicate joint possession, and to each of the names to show separate ownership.

Johnson and Hurstwood's; Haly, Scott & Wiggins'; Robley's and Tremmel's

g. The possessive pronouns (*his, hers, its, ours, yours, theirs,* and *whose*) do not require an apostrophe. But the possessive of the indefinite pronouns (*one's, either's, other's, someone's, somebody's,* etc.) is formed with an apostrophe.

his garden, her housework; one's rights, somebody's purse

Quotation Marks

14a. Use quotation marks to enclose a direct quotation.

"You are not yet of age, Ellen," her mother said.

Charles quickly replied, "This is an impressive argument, but it is quite beside the point."

b. If the quotation is broken by words of introduction or of comment, enclose each part of the broken quotation within quotation marks.

"The increase in profits," said the president, "is the result of lower selling costs and increased economy."

"What," he asked, "do you intend to do now?"

c. The insertion of words of introduction or comment does not change the original punctuation or capitalization of the quoted material. Punctuate independent clauses as independent clauses.

Wrong: "I shall be at home Tuesday," he said, "come to see me then."

Right: "I shall be at home Tuesday," he said; "come to see me then."

"I shall be at home Tuesday," he said. "Come to see me then."

d. In long quotations of several paragraphs, place quotation marks at the beginning of each paragraph but at the end of only the last one. Long quotations (over four lines) may be allowed to stand *without* quotation marks if they are single spaced and indented five spaces from the left margin.

e. A quotation within a quotation is enclosed in single quotation marks.

The officer said, "I warned the defendant that he was going too fast, but he shouted, 'Mind your own business.' "

f. In writing dialogue, enclose each separate speech within quotation marks, and make a new paragraph every time the speaker changes.

My grandfather snapped his fingers and said, "This is the very house I've been looking for."

"Some say it's haunted," whispered the landlord's daughter.

"The divil a bit do I care," replied my grandfather.

g. Place the comma and the period inside the quotation marks.

"Oh," you might say as you dash for the nearest exit, "you're trying to sell me life insurance."

h. Place the question mark and the exclamation point inside the quotation marks if they punctuate the

quoted material, and outside if they punctuate the whole sentence.

"Why should I be interested?" asked Curtis.

What did Curtis mean when he said, "I am not interested"?

i. Enclose in quotation marks quoted titles of articles, short stories, essays, chapters of books, short poems, booklets, and pamphlets.

Have you read the article entitled "Economic Distribution"?

Please read Poe's "The Pit and the Pendulum" to the class.

"Past and Present" is an essay, and "To a Skylark" is a delightful poem.

We are enclosing a copy of our booklet, "Eighty-five Ways to Make a Better Home."

j. Enclose in quotation marks technical terms, slang, nicknames, words used in a special way, or words to which particular attention is being called.

This Goodrich construction principle, the "shock-shield," has been proved in service over a period of years in the toughest of operations.

Esoteric means "secret."

How much money will be needed for "clean-up" expenses?

Italics

15a. Italicize titles of books, manuscripts, pictures, plays, musical compositions, motion pictures, magazines, newspapers, ships, docks, and airships. When a typewriter is used, italic type is indicated by an underscore.

The Grapes of Wrath, *Hamlet*, *Kansas City Blues*, *Cosmopolitan*, *Morning Oregonian*, the *Bremen*

b. Italicize words spoken of as words and letters considered as letters.

The greatest gift you can give your boy is an understanding of the word *thrift*.

In some styles of handwriting an *m* looks like a *w*.

c. Foreign words are usually italicized.

Our hats are *très chic*.

d. Italicize *RESOLVED* in formal resolutions.

RESOLVED: That American movies should not be censored.

The Question Mark

16a. A question mark follows a direct question.

Have you ever wished for a shirt that would make you look your best and yet be sturdy and practical enough for business wear?

"Will you call on us if we can be of assistance to you?" he asked.

b. A question mark placed in parentheses shows that the writer is doubtful of the correctness of a word, date, fact, or statement.

In 1480(?) François Villon, the greatest French poet of the Middle Ages, died.

The Exclamation Point

17. Use the exclamation point after words, phrases, or sentences to indicate strong feeling or surprise.

Why, I thought he was honest!

Five years! I may be dead and buried before that.

The Period

18a. A period marks the end of a declarative or an imperative sentence.

The order was shipped by air mail and will arrive in time for your special sale.

Look through the enclosed folder.

b. Place a period after an abbreviation.

Mr., Dr., Prof., Rev.

c. Do not place a period after a signature or after *Miss, per cent,* or Roman numerals.

Parentheses

19a. Enclose in parentheses explanatory, irrelevant, or foreign material inserted in the sentence.

The Safeguard Policy is easy to obtain (no medical examination is required), and it safeguards your earnings against the cost of accidents.

b. Enclose in parentheses explanatory figures, symbols, or words.

I shall send you a check for twenty dollars ($20) next week.

I shall send you a check for twenty (20) dollars next week.

Note: In typed letters it is unnecessary to repeat a written number or sum in figures enclosed in parentheses.

A substantive (noun) may be used as the direct object of a transitive verb.

c. Place punctuation marks after the parentheses.

If you are satisfied with the radio (and I am sure that you are), you may purchase it on easy terms.

Brackets

20. Brackets enclose notes or explanatory matter inserted by the writer in text that he is quoting or citing.

Our instructor said, "This story [*The Moon and Sixpence*] is the story of an English broker who leaves his wife, his home, and his position to go off to Paris to become a painter."

Capitals

21a. Capitalize the first word of every sentence, the first word of a direct quotation, and the first word of every line of poetry.

The salesman said, "This magazine is rich in articles and stories of unusual interest."

b. Capitalize proper nouns and adjectives.

(1) The names of persons and nouns that are personified.

Mary, William Wright, Joan of Arc, Vale of Tears, Mother Nature

(2) The names of days, months, holidays, and holy days.

Monday, June, Labor Day, Corpus Christi

(3) The names of historical events, movements, or epochs.

the Boston Tea Party, the French Revolution, the Renaissance, the Stone Age

(4) The names of organizations, institutions, foundations, clubs, firms, corporations, radio stations, labor unions, churches, and libraries.

Committee for Permanent Peace, Oregon Legislature, University of California, Carnegie Foundation, Underwood Corporation, Courtley, Ltd., KGW, American Federation of Labor, St. Mary's Church, Chicago Public Library

(5) The trade names of commercial articles.

Camels, Kleenex, Bon Ami, Listerine

(6) The names of streets, squares, parks, towers, monuments, statues, theaters, buildings, hotels, rooms, railway stations, platforms, trains, and cars.

Market Street, Grant Avenue, Washington Square, Lincoln Park, Tower of Pisa, the Washington Monument, the Granada Theater, Empress Hotel, Room Six, Illinois Central, the Red Arrow

(7) Names referring to languages or races.

French cooking, an Austrian peasant, the English language, American aggressiveness, Indian arrows

(8) Geographical names.

Vermont, the Pacific Northwest, Minneapolis, the Mojave Desert, Ireland, the Mississippi River, Elliot Bay, the Atlantic Ocean, Long Island

(9) The names of courts, boards, commissions, departments, agencies, and bureaus.

United States Supreme Court, New York Board of Trade, Interstate Commerce Commission, Department of Agriculture, Department of English, Bureau of Fisheries, Federal Security Agency

c. Capitalize the first word and all important words in the titles of books, magazines, newspapers, plays, motion pictures, radio programs, articles, essays, poems, musical compositions, reports, booklets, and pamphlets.

Lives of the English Poets, *The Saturday Evening Post*

d. Capitalize words referring to the Deity and to the Bible.

God, Christ, New Testament, Bible, Genesis

e. **Capitalize the first word of the salutation. Capitalize *dear* only when it is the first word.**

Dear Sir: My dear Sir: Dear Mr. Hoskins: Gentlemen:

f. **Capitalize only the first word of the complimentary close.**

Very truly yours, Sincerely yours, Yours respectfully,

g. **Miscellaneous uses:**

(1) **Capitalize the pronoun *I*.**

He asked if I would make a speech.

(2) **Capitalize titles standing before a proper name or used as a substitute for the name of a particular person.**

Dr. Thomas S. Schelling, Professor Markham, the President

(3) **Capitalize academic degrees and abbreviations of proper nouns.**

Ph.D., M.A., B.S., Bachelor of Arts, Doctor of Divinity, Va.

Personal names, like *Charles*, are never abbreviated. They should always be written in full.

(4) **Capitalize *WHEREAS* and *RESOLVED* in formal resolutions. Also capitalize the first word following *WHEREAS* or *RESOLVED*.**

RESOLVED: That the report . . .

(5) **Capitalize *the* if it is part of the proper name of a firm.**

The American Fur Company, The Second National Bank

(6) **Capitalize names of family relationship when used with proper names or when substituted for the name of a person.**

I asked Uncle Harry to persuade Mother to let me go.

My mother and father, as well as all my uncles, aunts, and cousins, gathered at Aunt Margaret's for the family reunion.

(7) **A.M. and P.M. may be either capitalized or written in small letters.**

h. Mistakes in capitalization:

(1) **Do not capitalize *ex-* when it is prefixed to a title.**

Right: Gloria read an article by ex-President Smith.

(2) **Do not capitalize the second member of a compound unless it is a proper noun or adjective.**

Right: Sixty-second Street, mid-Victorian

(3) **Do not capitalize the name of a study of a curriculum unless it is the name of a specific course or contains the name of a language or race.**

Right: English, Greek, mathematics, history, chemistry, Physics II, Economics III

(4) **Do not capitalize *freshman, sophomore, junior,* or *senior* when referring to a class in school.**

Right: the junior class, a freshman course

(5) **Do not capitalize certain nouns that are now considered common nouns:**

Right: chinaware, plaster of paris, morocco (leather), roman (type)

(6) **Do not capitalize the names of the seasons unless they are personified.**

Right:

Fill up your bin with Burnbrite coal before winter comes.

The fields were touched by the soft hand of Spring.

(7) Do not capitalize *east, west, north, south,* or any other direction considered merely as a direction. These words are capitalized only when they designate definite geographical sections of the country or when they are part of a company's name.

Right:

Walk two blocks north, and then go three east.

The cotton crop of the South; the Southwest; the East; the northern shore of France; the Pacific West Coast (or the West Coast); Western Fur Co.; Eastern Outfitters, Inc.

I like eastern oysters better than western.

Words

Proper Words

22a. Find the exact word to express your meaning. When in doubt, consult a dictionary.

Inexact: We appreciate your pointing out these *discrepancies* in our system.

Exact: We appreciate your pointing out these *faults* in our system.

Inexact: Punctuality is the first *axiom* of the exacting employer.

Exact: Punctuality is the first *requirement* of the exacting employer.

Inexact: A small sum will *yield* you a dependable watch.

Exact: A small sum will *buy* you a dependable watch.

Inexact: We are happy to extend *credit business* to new customers.

Exact: We are happy to extend *credit* to new customers.

b. Avoid slang and all other words not in current good usage.

Examples: complected, nowheres, gents, a try, humans, canines, swell, bully, get on the boat, I reckon, tote, wait on me, and how, enthuse

Words and Phrases to Avoid

23. Certain words and phrases are stereotyped. Others are negative and arouse unpleasant feelings in the reader.

The use of such words and phrases as *beg to advise, contents duly noted, kindly oblige, take the liberty* should be avoided.

Compound Words

24a. Insert a hyphen between two or more words standing as a single adjective before a noun.

self-evident fact, summer-grade oil, five-dollar hat, eight-inch pipe, up-to-date system, many-sided personality, so-called genius, twenty-dollar-a-week allowance, electro-dynamic speaker, diesel-electric locomotive, performance-proved engine, off-the-road tires, easy-to-read type

b. Hyphens should be used in compounds composed of a noun and a preposition or a prepositional phrase.

attorney-at-law, son-in-law, kick-off, hanger-on, sergeant-at-arms

c. Use a hyphen between the members of a compound noun when each member retains its identity; omit the hyphen if the nouns blend to form one idea.

actor-director, secretary-treasurer, taxpayer, baseball, storekeeper, cornfield

d. Hyphenate compound numbers below one hundred.

twenty-one, forty-six, sixty-three, ninety-nine

e. Place a hyphen between the numerator and the denominator of a fraction except when the numerator or the denominator is itself hyphenated.

four-fifths, three-ninths, forty-six hundredths, three twenty-sevenths

COMPOUND WORDS

f. Write the following words solid:

airship
already
altogether
anybody
anyone
anything
baseball
basketball
battleship
bedroom
birthday
blackberry
blackboard
blowout
blueprint
boathouse
bookkeeping
candlepower
cannot
childhood
classmate
correspondent
crankcase
daylight
daytime
downtown
everybody
everyone
everything
flywheel
football
foothill
foothold
foreman
furthermore
grandmother
halfpenny

halfway
handbook
handwriting
herself
himself
homelike
horsepower
iceberg
inasmuch
itself
lawgiver
lawsuit
letterhead
lifetime
lightweight
limelight
midnight
mudguard
myself
necktie
nevertheless
newspaper
nobody
nonexistent
noonday
nothing
nowadays
oilskin
oneself
overcharge
overdue
overlook
oversight
oversize
percentage
postmaster
quarterback

railroad
railway
rainfall
secondhand
semicolon
setscrew
shipyard
sidewalk
someone
somewhat
steamboat
stepfather
sunset
textbook
themselves
therefore
thumbprint
today
together
tomorrow
tonight
touchback
touchdown
toward
typewriter
typewritten
voltmeter
waterproof
whatsoever
wheelbase
wherever
withhold
workman
workshop
wristpin
yourself

g. Hyphenate the following words:

all-inclusive
all-out
by-law
by-product
double-barrelled
ex-president
first-class (*adj.*)
first-rate
four-in-hand
full-fledged
great-grandmother
half-breed
half-caste
half-mile
half-moon
half-tone
house-to-house (*adj.*)
left-handed
make-up
man-of-war
over-all
past-due (before a noun)
postage-paid
quarter-deck
ready-to-wear
right-handed
safe-keeping
self-addressed
self-satisfied
self-stamped
self-supporting
sight-seeing
snow-capped
take-off
time-saving
toss-up
un-American

h. Write the following words separate:

air compressor
all right
bank book
boiler room
cast iron
connecting rod
dining room
et cetera
fellow citizen
fellow employee
fellow passenger
fellow student
gas engine
good will
half brother
half pay
half price
half truth
in so far
life guard
night letter
no one
open house
parcel post
per cent
postal card
post office
power plant
real estate
rolling mill
rule of thumb
side line
side show
steam engine
steam turbine
street car
twist drill
water power
wing strut
worm gear

Plurals

25a. The plural of nouns is usually formed by adding *s* to the singular.

plan, plans; letter, letters; apple, apples; bell, bells

b. Nouns ending in *s, sh, ch, x,* or *z* add *es* to form the plural.

glass, glasses; rush, rushes; church, churches; box, boxes; quiz, quizzes

c. **Nouns ending in *y* preceded by a consonant form the plural by changing *y* to *i* and adding *es*.**

city, cities; comedy, comedies; lady, ladies

d. **Nouns ending in *y* preceded by a vowel add only *s*.**

boy, boys; valley, valleys; attorney, attorneys; key, keys

e. **Nouns ending in *o* preceded by a vowel form the plural by adding *s*.**

radio, radios; rodeo, rodeos; folio, folios

f. **Nouns ending in *o* preceded by a consonant form the plural by adding *s* or *es* (when in doubt, consult a dictionary).**

canto, cantos; dynamo, dynamos; halo, halos *or* haloes; memento, mementos *or* mementoes; quarto, quartos; piano, pianos; solo, solos; banjo, banjos; Navajo, Navajos *or* Navajoes; echo, echoes; cargo, cargos *or* cargoes; embargo, embargoes; motto, mottoes; potato, potatoes; hero, heroes; no, no's *or* noes; mosquito, mosquitoes; Negro, Negroes; tomato, tomatoes; mulatto, mulattoes; buffalo, buffalos *or* buffaloes

g. **The plural of some nouns ending in *f* or *fe* is formed by changing *f* or *fe* to *v* and adding *es*.**

life, lives; knife, knives; wife, wives; leaf, leaves; loaf, loaves; beef, beeves; thief, thieves; calf, calves; half, halves; elf, elves; shelf, shelves; self, selves; wolf, wolves; sheaf, sheaves

h. **A few nouns form the plural by adding *en* to the singular or by a change within the word.**

ox, oxen; child, children; goose, geese; foot, feet; mouse, mice; man, men; woman, women; tooth, teeth; louse, lice

i. The singular and plural of some nouns are the same.

deer, swine, trout, sheep, fish, moose

j. Many words derived from foreign languages retain their foreign plurals.

datum, data
index, indices (*or* indexes)
crisis, crises
alumnus, alumni
alumna, alumnæ
curriculum, curricula (*or* curriculums)
thesis, theses
phenomenon, phenomena
beau, beaux (*or* beaus)
fungus, fungi (*or* funguses)
focus, foci (*or* focuses)
radius, radii (*or* radiuses)
medium, media (*or* mediums)
stratum, strata (*or* stratums)
analysis, analyses
basis, bases
oasis, oases
parenthesis, parentheses
Mr., Messrs.
Mrs., Mesdames
formula, formulæ (*or* formulas)
hypothesis, hypotheses
memorandum, memoranda (*or* memorandums)

k. Compound nouns usually add *s* or *es* to the principal word of the combination.

fathers-in-law, attorneys-at-law, bystanders, passers-by
but, cupfuls, handfuls, menservants

l. Letters, figures, and signs form the plural by adding *'s*.

The word contained two *m's*. Too many *5's*. Six *&'s*.

Syllabication

26a. Divide words only between syllables. Place the hyphen at the end of the line, not at the beginning of the next line.

func-tion, con-sign, fran-chise, super-intendent, traf-fic, trans-fer, re-spond

b. Words of one syllable cannot be divided.

man, haste, through, sixth, rouge, bring, drought

c. Divide two consonants that are pronounced in different syllables.

plun-der, for-mal, ful-fil, fac-tory, con-sider

d. Place the hyphen before or after a single consonant between vowels so that the consonant is put with the vowel with which it is pronounced.

pro-vide, shad-ow, mead-ow, ordi-nance, fa-cial

e. Of a group of three consonants, keep together those consonants that are pronounced together.

dis-charge, demon-strate, par-tridge, dis-criminate, rum-ple, con-scious, frank-ness

f. Divide compounds between the component members.

grand-mother, battle-ship, well-known, self-sacrifice

g. Prefixes and suffixes are divided from the rest of the word.

amuse-ment, force-ful, dis-appear, ante-cedent, un-wise, sick-ness, under-nourished, trans-atlantic

h. Ordinarily do not separate one or two letters (except prefixes and suffixes) from the rest of the word.

around, busy, burned, along, equal, erupt

Abbreviations

27a. As a general rule, avoid abbreviations. Write out words in full.

Wrong: blk., cap., reg., bu., bbl.
Right: black, capital, registered, bushel, barrel

b. It is proper to abbreviate *Mr.; Mrs.; Messrs.; A. M.; P. M.; A. D.; B. C.;* methods of shipment, such as *F. O. B.;* and terms of sale.

c. It is permissible to use the abbreviations *Dr.*, *Hon.*, *Prof.*, and *Rev.* when they precede a person's name. Degrees, such as *Ph.D.*, *D.D.*, and *M.A.*, are abbreviated when they follow a proper name.

Dr. Henry Schell, Prof. H. S. Swope, Rev. John M. Wadsworth, Martin Rickard, Ph.D.

d. The following are the proper abbreviations of academic degrees:

A.B. or B.A.	Bachelor of Arts
A.M. or M.A.	Master of Arts
B. Arch.	Bachelor of Architecture
B.C.E.	Bachelor of Civil Engineering
B.C.L.	Bachelor of Civil Law
B.D.	Bachelor of Divinity
B.L.	Bachelor of Law
B.Litt.	Bachelor of Literature or Bachelor of Letters
B.Mus. or Mus.B.	Bachelor of Music
B.S.	Bachelor of Science
C.E.	Civil Engineer
C.P.A.	Certified Public Accountant
D.D.	Doctor of Divinity
D.D.S.	Doctor of Dental Surgery
D.Ed.	Doctor of Education
D.Litt. or Litt.D.	Doctor of Literature or Doctor of Letters
D.M.D.	Doctor of Dental Medicine
D.Mus.	Doctor of Music
D.Sc.	Doctor of Science
D.V.M.	Doctor of Veterinary Medicine
E.E.	Electrical Engineer
J.D.	Doctor of Jurisprudence
LL.B.	Bachelor of Laws
LL.D.	Doctor of Laws
M.D.	Doctor of Medicine
Ph.B.	Bachelor of Philosophy
Ph.D.	Doctor of Philosophy
Ph.G.	Graduate in Pharmacy
R.N.	Registered Nurse

e. Spell out all titles that are used alone.

Right: Professor, Doctor, Manager, President, Captain, General, Superintendent

f. Do not abbreviate the names of months, states, countries, or persons.

Wrong: Jun., O., Can., Jno.
Right: June, Ohio, Canada, John

g. Avoid abbreviating the words *Street, Avenue, Railroad, Mountain, Road, Brothers, Park,* and *Building.*

Wrong: Maple St., Southern Pacific R.R., Cascade Mts., Central Pk., State-Lake Bldg.

Right: Maple Street, Southern Pacific Railroad, Cascade Mountains, Central Park, State-Lake Building

h. Never use such abbreviations as *D'r., Y'rs., S'r., Sinc'ly., Resp., Gents., ad., and etc.,* 3/18/51. Do not use & or *Co.* unless it is officially so written in the name of a firm. Do not use such signs as # / " for abbreviations for *pounds, per,* or *inches.*

Numbers

28a. In the body of the letter, spell out isolated numbers that can be expressed in one or two words; use figures for all other numbers.

Correct: Five; two hundred; three thousand; one million; 6,748; 1,269,152.

Note: If the letter contains many numbers, use figures for all the numbers except those that begin sentences. Spell out the first of two consecutive numbers; *e.g.*, two 60-h.p. motors.

b. Do not use *d, nd, rd, st,* or *th* after the number of the day. However, when the month is not mentioned or when the day precedes the month, either these abbreviations or ordinal numbers may be used.

Wrong:
February 3rd, 1951
The order was shipped on April 21st.

Right:

February 3, 1951
The order was shipped on April 21.
We received your order on the eighth of May.
Your letter of the 16th contained no remittance.

c. Do not abbreviate the date.

Wrong:	*Right:*
7/18/51	July 18, 1951
7–18–51	1951
7–18–'51	
'51	

d. Spell out the numeric names of streets and avenues if they are composed of single numbers; express them in figures if they are compounds.

Right:

Sixth Street
Second Avenue
Thirtieth Street
Tenth Avenue
83rd Street
61st Street
142nd Street
East 155 Street

e. Place the postal delivery zone number after the city and separate it from the state by a comma.

Cleveland 7, Ohio

Following is a list of post offices using the postal zone number system. The numbers included as part of addresses under this system are referred to as postal delivery zone numbers. The numbers designate delivery units of zones within the limits of delivery of a particular post office. There has been no delivery zone number assigned for addressing mail to The White House, the United States Senate, or the U. S. House of Representatives. Such mail is correctly addressed to Washington, D. C., without any zone number. All mail going to Federal Government agencies in Washington, D. C., is addressed to Zone 25 (*e.g.*, The War Department, The Secretary of State, The Attorney General, The Bureau of Education). Mail for the U. S. Supreme Court is addressed to Washington 13, D. C.

Alabama
Birmingham
Mobile
Montgomery
California
Berkeley
Fresno
Glendale
Hollywood
Long Beach
Los Angeles
Oakland
Pasadena
Sacramento
San Diego
San Francisco
San Jose
Stockton
Colorado
Denver
Connecticut
Bridgeport
Hartford
New Haven
Waterbury
Delaware
Wilmington
District of Columbia
Washington
Florida
Jacksonville
Miami
St. Petersburg
Tampa
Georgia
Atlanta
Territory of Hawaii
Honolulu
Illinois
Chicago
Decatur
Peoria
Indiana
Evansville
Fort Wayne
Indianapolis
South Bend
Iowa
Des Moines
Sioux City
Kansas
Kansas City
Wichita
Kentucky
Lexington
Louisville
Louisiana
Alexandria
Baton Rouge
New Orleans
Shreveport
Maine
Portland
Maryland
Baltimore
Massachusetts
Boston
Brockton
Springfield
Worcester
Michigan
Detroit
Flint
Grand Rapids
Kalamazoo
Lansing
Pontiac
Minnesota
Duluth
Minneapolis
St. Paul
Mississippi
Jackson
Missouri
Kansas City
St. Joseph
St. Louis
Nebraska
Lincoln
Omaha
New Jersey
Elizabeth

[28]

WORDS

Jersey City
Newark
Paterson
Trenton

New York

Albany
Brooklyn
Buffalo
Jamaica
Long Island City
New York
Rochester
Schenectady
Staten Island
Syracuse
Utica
Yonkers

North Carolina

Charlotte
Winston-Salem

Ohio

Akron
Canton
Cincinnati
Cleveland
Columbus
Dayton
Toledo
Youngstown

Oklahoma

Oklahoma City
Tulsa

Oregon

Portland

Pennsylvania

Philadelphia
Pittsburgh
Scranton
Williamsport

Puerto Rico

San Juan

Rhode Island

Providence

South Carolina

Charleston
Columbia

Tennessee

Chattanooga
Knoxville
Memphis
Nashville

Texas

Austin
Dallas
Fort Worth
Houston
San Antonio

Utah

Salt Lake City

Virginia

Norfolk
Richmond
Roanoke

Washington

Seattle
Spokane
Tacoma

West Virginia

Charleston
Huntington

Wisconsin

Madison
Milwaukee

f. Use figures to express sums of money consisting of both dollars and cents.

Right: $19.36

g. Write out amounts in cents.

Right: twenty cents; ninety-eight cents

h. Omit both the decimal point and the zeroes if the amount denotes even dollars.

Right: $960

i. In typed letters, one form of writing a sum of money is sufficient.

Superfluous: forty-six dollars ($46)

Correct: forty-six dollars *or* $46

j. Do not begin a sentence with figures.

Wrong: 62 cases were shipped during March.

Right: Sixty-two cases were shipped during March.

k. Roman numerals are used in referring to chapters of books, articles of documents, acts of plays, and names of rulers.

Right:
Chapter IV, p. 46
Article XII, Section 9
Act III, scene ii, line 32 (better: III, ii, 32)
Job XIV: 2–4
Henry IV

l. When the number is part of a proper name identifying a room, place, or other thing, do not spell out the number unless it is officially written out in the name.

Right: Platform 6, Platform Six, Locker 27, Locker Twenty-seven, District 14, Apartment 9

m. Do not spell out dates, house numbers, page numbers, or telephone numbers.

Right: October 2, 1951; 874 Maple Street; page 50; Englewood 1194

n. Write out fractions.

Right: four-fifths; six-sevenths; three twenty-seconds

o. Decimals with no units should have a cipher before the decimal point.

Right: The specified diameter shall be 0.35 inch.

Grammar

Verbs

29a. A verb agrees with its subject in person and number.

The billing and control *system*, with its division of accounts into alphabetical groups and its establishment of controls for each group, *eliminates* itemizing.

The yard's *records show* that each diesel-electric *locomotive uses* only three gallons of fuel an hour.

There *are* other advertising *plans* in the portfolio.

Although *I am* never *tired*, *he is* easily *fatigued.*

This *kind* of story *interests* me.

b. ***Each, every, everyone, someone, everybody, anybody, anyone, no one, nobody, one, either,*** **and** ***neither*** **take singular verbs.**

Either of the plans *is* acceptable.

One of the applicants *is* well qualified.

Everybody wants a job.

c. Two or more subjects joined by *and* take a plural verb.

The sale and distribution of our product in your territory *are* under the supervision of our regional office in Denver.

Typewriters and comptometers *are* useful machines.

But when the compound subject consists of two nouns referring to the same person or thing, the verb is singular.

His wife and companion *is* dead.

d. Singular subjects joined by *or, nor, and not, but, either . . . or,* or *neither . . . nor* take singular verbs.

Neither the sales manager nor the auditor *was* present at the meeting.

Salt *or* soda *is* good for the teeth.

No one *but* a member *is* eligible.

e. Collective nouns take singular verbs to express collective action, and plural verbs to express individual action.

The council *disagrees* with the mayor.

The council *disagree* among themselves.

f. Learn the principal parts of the following irregular verbs:

Present	*Past*	*Past Participle*
arise	arose	arisen
begin	began	begun
bid	bid	bid
bid	bade	bidden
blow	blew	blown
break	broke	broken
bring	brought	brought
broadcast	broadcast	broadcast
burst	burst	burst
catch	caught	caught
choose	chose	chosen
come	came	come
dive	dived	dived
do	did	done
drink	drank	drunk
drive	drove	driven
drown	drowned	drowned
eat	ate	eaten
fall	fell	fallen
flow	flowed	flowed
fly	flew	flown
forecast	forecast	forecast
forget	forgot	forgotten

Present	*Past*	*Past Participle*
freeze	froze	frozen
get	got	got
grow	grew	grown
hang	hung	hung
hang (*execute*)	hanged	hanged
know	knew	known
lay (*put*)	laid	laid
lead	led	led
lend	lent	lent
lie (*recline*)	lay	lain
lie	lied	lied
mean	meant	meant
pay	paid	paid
plead	pleaded	pleaded
prove	proved	proved (en)
ride	rode	ridden
ring	rang	rung
rise	rose	risen
run	ran	run
see	saw	seen
set	set	set
shake	shook	shaken
shine	shone	shone
show	showed	shown
shrink	shrank	shrunk
sing	sang	sung
sink	sank	sunk
sit	sat	sat
sleep	slept	slept
sow	sowed	sown, sowed
speak	spoke	spoken
spend	spent	spent
stay	stayed	stayed
steal	stole	stolen
sting	stung	stung
strike	struck	struck
swear	swore	sworn
swim	swam	swum
swing	swung	swung

Present	*Past*	*Past Participle*
take	took	taken
tear	tore	torn
throw	threw	thrown
wake	woke, waked	woke, waked
wear	wore	worn
weave	wove	woven
win	won	won
wind	wound	wound
wring	wrung	wrung
write	wrote	written

Pronouns

30a. Use pronouns correctly. The nominative case (*I, he, she, we, they, who, whoever*) is used as subject and predicate nominative. The objective case (*me, him, her, us, them, whom, whomever*) is used as the object of a verb or a preposition.

Jones and *I* represent this company.

The sales manager promoted Jones and *me*.

He gave the order to *her* (*him, them, me, us*).

It was *I* (*she, he, we, they*).

If you were *I* (*he, she, we, they*), would you accept the order?

The prize will be given to *whoever* has the best record.

Whom did you see at the convention?

For *whom* did you vote?

b. Avoid faulty reference of pronouns. The noun to which the pronoun refers must be unmistakably clear.

Faulty reference: We again notice that you have failed to pay your account with us. You have had the privilege of charging *it*.

Clear: You have again failed to pay your account with us. You have had the privilege of charging *purchases*.

Faulty reference: This accommodation is made possible by the coöperation of each person in meeting *their* obligations promptly, or in giving an explanation of why *they* are not punctual.

Clear: This accommodation is possible only through the coöperation of each person in meeting *his* obligations promptly or in explaining why *he* is not punctual.

c. The pronoun must agree with its antecedent in gender and number.

Right: Everyone in the sales department is expected to make *his* report by Saturday.

Both the president and the treasurer have completed *their* reports.

Joan will submit *her* report tomorrow.

d. *Who* and *whose* refer to persons. *Which* refers to animals and things. *That* refers to persons, animals, or things.

Right: The angry customer asked for the salesman *who* had sold him the battery.

The boxes *which* were shipped from Cleveland arrived in good condition.

The man *that* just applied for credit is a good risk.

The horse *that* I bought was lame.

e. The noun or pronoun to which the relative pronoun (*who, which,* or *that*) refers must be contained within the sentence.

Right: The *sales letter* which the secretary wrote produced good results.

Wrong: He did his work well, which pleased the manager.

Right: Because he did his work well, the manager was pleased.

Modifiers

31a. Place modifiers near or next to the words they modify. The sentence is incorrect if a word, phrase, or clause seems to modify a word that the writer did not intend to be so modified.

Wrong: Smith's automobile broke down on *Ninth Street,* which the mechanic had repaired.

Right: Smith's *automobile,* which the mechanic had repaired, broke down on Ninth Street.

Wrong: He could see the parade *coming* down the street through his office window.

Right: Through his office window, he *could see* the parade coming down the street.

Misplaced modifier: The credit manager *told* Smith when the proper time came he *would grant* him credit. (Does *when the proper time came* modify *told* or *would grant?*)

Clear: The credit manager told Smith that he *would grant* him credit when the proper time came.

b. See that every participle modifies a noun or pronoun within the sentence. Guard against referring an action to the wrong agent.

Wrong: After posting the sales journal, *the books* were closed.

Right: After the sales journal *was posted,* the books were closed.

Wrong: Answering your inquiry, the *five-ton truck* will be delivered to you on March 17.

Right: Answering your inquiry, *we* assure you that the five-ton truck will be delivered to you on March 17.

Wrong: Burned to a crisp, the *housewife* removed the biscuits from the oven.

Right: The housewife removed the *biscuits,* which were burned to a crisp, from the oven.

c. Place *only, ever, almost,* and *at least* near the words they modify and where they express exactly what is meant.

Wrong: The credit manager *only* inquired about these three accounts.

Right: The credit manager inquired about *only* these three accounts.

Wrong: The Writewell fountain pen will *almost* give perfect satisfaction.

Right: The Writewell fountain pen will give *almost* perfect satisfaction.

d. Do not confuse adjectives and adverbs. Make every adjective modify a noun. Make every adverb modify a verb, an adjective, or another adverb.

Sentences

32a. Every sentence must have a subject and a predicate in the form of an independent clause and must make complete sense. Do not set off a part of a sentence as if it were a complete thought.

Wrong: Your order having been sent last Tuesday. (This is only a phrase, not a sentence.)

Since your order was sent last Tuesday. (This is a subordinate clause only. Because there is no independent clause, the group of words is not a sentence.)

Right: Since your order was sent last Tuesday, it should arrive on Saturday, June 15. (This is a complete sentence because it contains an independent clause.)

Note: In advertisements and sales letters, and in these only, it is permissible to use fragments when the writer wishes to secure highly special effects.

b. Do not run together two or more complete sentences as if they were one. Set off complete statements by a period or semicolon.

Wrong: Refresh your skin each day with an astringent the tonic effect will be stimulating.

Refresh your skin each day with an astringent, the tonic effect will be stimulating.

Right: Refresh your skin each day with an astringent. The tonic effect will be stimulating.

c. Do not cut up logically related statements into short, jerky sentences.

Poor: We are investigating certain conditions. We believe that these exist in the teaching profession. We want to complete intelligently our analysis. It is necessary that we secure additional information.

Good: We are investigating certain conditions which we believe exist in the teaching profession. In order that we may intelligently complete our analysis, it is necessary that we secure additional information.

d. Long, stringy sentences made up of clauses connected by *and* and *but* are ineffective. Break up stringy sentences into shorter sentences or subordinate the less important material.

Poor: Our company sold six oil burners to John Rogers *and* he manages the largest store in Pocatello *and* this is his home town.

Good: Our company sold six oil burners to John Rogers. He manages the largest store in Pocatello, his home town.

Our company sold six oil burners to John Rogers, who manages the largest store in Pocatello, his home town.

e. Coördinate only ideas of equal importance. Subordinate minor ideas.

Good: Come in any time. We shall be glad to help you.

Poor: You will soon be ready to buy, and we suggest that you look for the U.S.S. label on these products.

The Yale article will interest you more than those that follow, and we are sure that you will enjoy every one of them.

Good: When you are ready to buy, we suggest that you look for the U.S.S. label on these products.

Although the Yale article will interest you more than those that follow, we are sure that you will enjoy every one of them.

Poor: Your outboard motor has been thoroughly overhauled and tested in our factory, so you may be sure of satisfactory performance.

Good: Because your outboard motor has been thoroughly overhauled and tested in our factory, you may be sure of satisfactory performance.

f. Express parallel (similar) ideas in parallel grammatical form. Avoid a shift in construction.

Wrong: Paying bills promptly is better than to put them off.

Right: Paying bills promptly is better than putting them off.

Wrong: The Black Company sells rugs of beauty and having durability.

Right: The Black Company sells rugs of beauty and of durability (*or* beautiful and durable rugs).

Wrong: The applicant was told to appear for a personal interview and that he must bring samples of his work.

Right: The applicant was told to appear for a personal interview and to bring samples of his work.

Wrong: The president made his speech forcefully, persuasively, and with tact.

Right: The president made his speech forcefully, persuasively, and tactfully.

g. The sentences of the letter should be correct, effective, and clear. They should be of uninvolved construction and of varied length.

No other tire has been so favorably thought of for so long a time.

Dealers must keep pace with the times.

Homes that are built for sale must have features of particular interest to the prospective buyer.

For your convenience an order card is enclosed.

The results of this investigation have been utilized in developing Anaconda Condenser Tubes to their present state of perfection.

h. Although sentence length is a matter of adaptation to the reader, to the purpose of the message, and to the character of the house, business sentences tend to be short.

Your neighborhood druggist has Lifebuoy Shaving Cream.

The coming holiday season presents unusual opportunity for premium activities.

It is novel. It is new. It is an experience most haven't had.

Please let us hear from you within the next ten days.

i. Short sentences are effective in sales letters, collection letters, or other letters the purpose of which is to stimulate action. They are also commonly used at the beginning and the end of letters.

Try it and see!

How many would you like to have?

Where this plan has been used, an increase of ten per cent has not been unusual.

You work from early to late to get the best returns from your business. Yet you do not make the profit you should.

Won't you do your part and remit now?

Please don't put it off this time. Just pin your check for $39.84 to this letter and mail it now. We are looking for it.

j. Long sentences may be used in answers to claims, letters refusing credit, letters aiming to conciliate the reader, and letters in which care is taken to avoid offense or irritation. They may be used to give the effect of dignity and conservatism.

We're confident that Mr. Adams won't expect us to do all this remodeling for nothing, but we want to make sure. We could just wash and polish that old "car," place it in perfect running condition, and not charge a dime for the work, but we would really rather have Mr. Adams perfectly satisfied.

Although at all times we try to ship our orders as promptly as possible, sometimes we have difficulty in doing so because of the fact that we carry a limited stock to insure the freshness of our candies when shipped.

In all, it will be brought to the attention of more than 4,500,000 people, who have been told repeatedly of the advantages of rustless copper, brass, and bronze through Anaconda's consistent advertising during the past ten years.

k. The sentences of a letter should be clear not only in themselves, but also in relation to those that precede and follow.

Coherent: Nation-wide advertising during the past ten years has created a preference for Anaconda Copper. It will be to your advantage to tie in with this advertising by using the free folders and blotters we offer. Order your supply today before you forget it. For your convenience, an order card is enclosed.

Incoherent: Do you envy your friends' seemingly inexhaustible supply of novel ideas for beautifying the home and garden? Wouldn't you like to know about the beauty spots of the West where you can spend your vacation? Naturally you hate to have your home look inferior to someone else's. Nor do you want your garden to appear unkempt and unattractive when compared with others.

l. The structure of the sentence is determined by the idea to be expressed, the tone, and the emotional effect desired.

m. The simple sentence contains one independent clause. It is best suited to the expression of a simple thought.

We find your account still unpaid.

Of course, I immediately recognized the account as that of an old and valued customer.

Sixty-two stations in one day is a record for any radio.

n. The compound sentence contains two or more independent clauses; it is effective for the expression of independent ideas intimately related.

Send us the handy postcard at once, and we'll gladly send you a portfolio of business forms used by others in your kind of business.

Consult with the head of the make-up department in your own studio, or call at our studios in Hollywood for complete information.

Public acceptance means public patronage; it means more sales, quicker sales, and easier sales.

o. The complex sentence, which contains one independent clause and one or more dependent clauses, shows the precise relationships between ideas of unequal importance.

When he delivers these samples, our representative will welcome an opportunity to offer suggestions on any of your filing problems.

If you are going abroad, allow us to make your reservation during the next few weeks to insure the best accommodations at the minimum cost.

They will tell you what other people are doing.

We hope that you will find it convenient to adhere to these terms.

You will find the Tax Manual, which is now in the process of preparation, the best six-dollar investment in tax information that you have ever made.

p. If the thought of the sentence is not complete until the end of the sentence is reached, the sentence is periodic. Periodic sentences may be used to produce a dignified, conservative tone.

Harsh mouth washes, aping Halatol, often do irritate.

Undoubtedly you are planning to have the heating plant in your new house automatically controlled.

There is no more appreciative article that you can offer your customers than a Tiny Tim.

q. The loose sentence is one in which the reader gets the meaning before the end of the sentence is reached.

These recipes are the creation of the noted Betty Crocker, distinguished Gold Medal expert.

Fast trains bring you here quickly, without extra fare.

The temperature of electric refrigeration is automatically controlled and set below fifty degrees for the protection of food and health.

r. A balanced sentence is one in which the similarity or contrast of the thoughts is emphasized by repetition of the grammatical construction.

If it isn't Armco Ingot Iron, it isn't rust-resistant.

The purer the base metal, the better the coating.

Think of Sterling and you think of Silver; think of Silvertown and you think of Goodrich.

s. The structure of the sentences must be varied to avoid monotony, to make the letter pleasant to read, and to secure accuracy of expression.

Why not break away from routine and come to Portland for a few days of change and recreation that will do you a world of good? You can have the time of your life at Jantzen Beach with its marvelous swimming pools, its scores of thrilling rides, its great dance pavilion, and its beautiful grounds. In the evenings, you can see first-run motion pictures at Portland's magnificent theaters. Then, too, Portland's stores are showing their new fall styles.

t. Emphasis in both the paragraph and the sentence lies at the beginning and the end. Emphasis may also be secured by contrast, repetition, and diction.

Max Factor, with his twenty years of practical and technical experience, is ably qualified to assist you and your students.

Where is there a name in the tire industry equal to the name of Silvertown?

They remain taut and firm, new in appearance, and they are *not expensive.*

Paragraphs

33a. A paragraph presents a single topic or idea clearly, concisely, and completely. It is a unit representing a natural break or a logical division of the thought. Each paragraph makes a definite step forward toward the objective of the letter. Since there are no fixed rules for paragraphing business letters, the writer must use his own judgment in dividing and subdividing his topics.

Dear Mr. White:

The booklet that you requested has been mailed to you.

You will enjoy this "different" presentation of a "different" type of accounting machine—the new Completely Electrified Remington.

The machine actually institutes new methods of accomplishing accounting work. The "short cuts" permitted by the application of electricity to the machine operation result in great savings of time, effort, and money—always, you will agree, advantages that appeal to alert and progressive business men.

You have but to say the word, and our representative will gladly show you how the economies made possible by this new Remington may be brought to your own accounting. His visit will not obligate you in any way.

Very truly yours,

REMINGTON RAND BUSINESS SERVICE, INC.

b. **Paragraphs may be used for display purposes. An important sentence is emphasized by being written as a separate paragraph.**

This is the spot where protection should start—right where the sale is recorded.

The price of the Filer is just $69.

BALANCE in pens is just yours and SHEAFFER'S to sell.

ARE YOU ACCIDENT PROOF?

You owe us $19.63.

c. **In business letters, a paragraph may be a mechanical unit or a structural unit.** As a mechanical unit, the paragraph is a pleasing division of the black and white spaces of the letter. As a structural or thought unit, the paragraph represents the effective development of a single topic or idea. The structural paragraph may be developed in the following ways:

1. From the general to the particular.
2. From the particular to the general.
3. From result to cause.
4. By comparison and contrast.
5. By specific details.
6. By parallel construction.
7. By repetition.
8. By climactic order.

d. Paragraph length is adapted to the reader, the material, and the length of the whole letter. However, paragraphs in business letters tend to be short.

Goodrich is also, we believe, better equipped and better organized to meet new forms of competition than any other company in the field.

Learn all you can about our product and how it will benefit our users. If you will do this, your success will be in direct proportion to the number of hours you work and the number of people on whom you call.

As part of this year's Screen Wire Advertising, we have prepared the enclosed sales help material for manufacturers of Custom Screens. We will supply this material to you, in quantity, free of charge, with your firm name and address imprinted on every copy. These mailing pieces will uncover many valuable leads and pave the way for worthwhile calls.

These are the things we offer for your greater shaving comfort. We worked eighteen months to attain them, testing one hundred and thirty formulas so that you might shave with enjoyment.

e. Short paragraphs are brisk, stimulating, and reveal the meaning quickly. They speed up the letter. Short paragraphs are nearly always used at the beginnings and endings of sales letters.

This sample of Ingram's Shaving Cream brings you seven of the COOLEST shaves you've ever had in your life!

The plan proved such a remarkable success that we are passing it along to you . . . all worked out in detail, ready for you to put into immediate use.

If you are interested in learning how this method will apply to your business and save you money, time, and worry, mail the postcard.

f. Longer paragraphs demand a more deliberate reading. They are well adapted to educated and conservative readers, to letters that aim to conciliate readers, to formal letters, and to reports.

Our edition was made by the well-known firm of Max Jaffe, in Vienna. It is thoroughly reliable and accurate, so that it may be used for all purposes of study and reference. Furthermore, as one noted Shakespeare scholar has written us, it reproduces to a surprising extent the general feeling and atmosphere of the original. Every student and lover of Shakespeare will find it a valuable addition to his collection.

Your order was delayed because of the pecan rolls which you ordered. Since these are much better when they are fresh, we purposely do not carry many of them in stock. The manufacture of these rolls is somewhat slow. It is necessary for the centers to be made one day and allowed to stand until the next. Then the pecans are put on two sides, but a couple of hours must elapse before they are put on the other two sides. Finally, the rolls must become thoroughly dry before they are wrapped in cellophane.

g. Vary paragraph length and structure and avoid extremes.

Dear Mr. Houk:

You will find "Catalogs that Sell" good reading. We are sending it to you promptly, as you asked.

Sales executives in your kind of business usually find the suggestions on page four of particular interest. Why not turn to page four first? These ideas ought to be worth adopting right in your own company.

You'll find the entire booklet packed full of sound selling sense. Some of these points you will want to discuss with the Remington Rand man. Ask him to bring in some samples of salesmen's and general catalog covers adapted specially to your business. His visit will not obligate you in any way.

We appreciate the interest that prompted your inquiry and will be glad to help you in any way we can with the covers of your catalogs.

Very truly yours,

REMINGTON RAND BUSINESS SERVICE, INC.

Exact Connectives

34a. Use the proper connectives wherever it is necessary to make clear the connection between sentences and between paragraphs. Choose the connective that shows the exact relationship between the thoughts. Distinguish between coördinating connectives (those that link ideas of equal value) and subordinating connectives (those that join ideas of unequal value). Distinguish also between those connectives that indicate a similar line of thought, and those that express contrast. Choose the proper connective to denote time, place, cause, manner, comparison, condition, concession, purpose, or result.

accordingly	certainly	in any case
after	consequently	inasmuch as
again	disregarding that	in case that
also	equally important	indeed
although	especially	in fact
and	even if	in order that
anyhow	ever since	in particular
as	except that	in spite of
as a consequence	finally	in truth
as an alternative	first	in view of this
as a result	for	just as
as . . . as	for example	lastly
as if	for instance	lest
as long as	for that reason	likewise
as often as	for the purpose of	meanwhile
as soon as	for the sake of	more effective
as though	for this purpose	moreover
at any rate	further	more than
at last	furthermore	naturally
at least	hence	nevertheless
because	however	next
before	if	not so obvious
besides	if ever	not that
but	if only	notwithstanding
but that	in addition	now

now consider
of course
on condition that
on the contrary
on the other hand
on the whole
otherwise
prior to
provided
provided that
quite as necessary
rather than
really
secondly
similarly
since
so
so . . . as
so that
specifically
such . . . that
surely
than
that
that's why
the more . . . the more
then
therefore
thereupon
thirdly
though
thus
till
to be sure
to bring about
too
to this end
truly
unless
until
when
whence
whenever
where
whereas
wherever
whereupon
which
while
whither
with a view to
with this in view
yet

b. The following examples illustrate the proper use of connectives and transitions:

This sturdily constructed, moderately priced line consists of nine popular styles. Additional combinations are *also* possible through the use of the substitute drawer inserts mentioned in the attached folder. *Yet* you will find the Art Metal "6700" Lines as handsome and sturdy in every way as more expensive files.

We have been very lenient in writing you about your contract note. *However*, four bills and three letters have failed to bring a remittance.

Perhaps your remittance has been temporarily delayed and is now on the way. *In that event*, the amount will be credited promptly when received.

Frankly, we are reluctant to send your account to our lawyer for collection. *After all*, while lawyers do have a way of getting money in the end, legal recourse is expensive and often leads to many unpleasant consequences. *Accordingly*, we are going to give you every chance to avoid outside collection of your account.

Now we request your immediate attention to the matter, and we frankly ask that you send a check without further delay. *In making this request,* we feel that we are asking for nothing more than that to which you consider us fairly entitled.

A complete system with the Filer, 5,000 sets of tickets in triplicate of the smaller size, with carbon paper and post binders, costs just $97.75. *Of course,* the cost per thousand forms is much less when you buy larger quantities.

Comparisons

35a. Do not make incomplete comparisons. They are confusing.

Not clear: He likes our Super-Knit goods better than our competitors'.

Clear: He likes our Super-Knit goods better than our competitors' knitted goods.

b. Compare similar things—an object with an object, a person with a person, a quality with a quality, and so forth.

Wrong: The efficiency of this machine is greater than a steam engine.

Right: The efficiency of this machine is greater than *that of* a steam engine.

c. Compare a thing with *any other* thing of its own class.

Wrong: I like this watch better than any in your display.

Right: I like this watch better than any *other* in your display.

d. Compare a thing with *any* thing of a class *not* its own.

Right: I like this watch better than *any watch* in your competitor's line.

Correlatives

36. Use correlatives, *both . . . and, either . . . or, neither . . . nor, not only . . . but also,* and *whether . . . or,* to connect ideas logically related. See that they are followed by similar grammatical elements—a noun and a noun, a verb and a verb, a phrase and a phrase, and so forth.

Wrong: You must either *send* your check or your *note.*

Right: You must send either your *check* or your *note.*

Wrong: This antiseptic is not only *effective* but also *of low price.*

Right: This antiseptic is not only *effective* but also *inexpensive.*

Qualities

Clearness

37a. Make the letter so clear that it cannot be misunderstood.

Involved and fuzzy:

Gentlemen:

Replying to your letter of October 15, with reference to our carload shipment of September 11, in which you received a five-gallon can of Collodion with a nail driven into the can through the wooden case, which resulted in contents leaking out and running down onto a couple cases of 11 by 14 Dupli-Tized X-Ray Film Super Speed in six dozen packages, staining fifteen of the boxes; wish to advise that the cartons for the Film were shipped to you by parcel post on October 27, which we hope you will receive without delay.

We regret very much the accident of the nail being driven through the case. We have called it to the attention of the shippers of this material and asked them to be very careful on future shipments.

Very truly yours,[1]

Clear:

Gentlemen:

We regret very much to hear of the damage caused by the punctured can of Collodion, to which you referred in your letter of October 15. On October 27 we sent you by express another can of Collodion and new cartons to replace those which were damaged.

We thank you for telling us about it, as this experience will prompt us to use greater care in future shipments.

Very truly yours,[2]

[1] From *Writing Kodak Letters*, Eastman Kodak Company.
[2] *Ibid.*

b. Express yourself in correct rhetorical and grammatical form. Use effective sentences, simple and familiar words, and uninvolved constructions.

c. Adapt the language and the tone of the letter to the reader.

d. Be sure that the letter is complete.

e. The letter will be clear if the writer knows his product and his reader, if he has clearly in mind the purpose of the letter, the response he wishes to get and how he is going to get it, and if he has logically thought out and planned the letter.

Correctness

38a. The business letter should be truthful and accurate in its presentation of facts and information. It must conform to the accepted standards of letter writing.

b. The letter must be correct in its physical make-up, that is, choice of paper stock, size of sheet, letterhead, headings of the letter and their arrangement, and all details involved in the distribution of the material on the sheet. (See the sections on Letter Dress, **1–8**.)

c. Correctness in usage, language, and the mechanical details of expression is important. Errors in spelling, punctuation, capitalization, grammar, and sentence structure annoy the reader and create a negative impression. (See the sections on Punctuation and Capitals, **9–21**, Words, **22–28**, and Grammar, **29–36**.)

Consideration—The *You* Attitude

39a. Write the letter from the viewpoint of the reader. Show him of what advantage the product or the service is

to him. Consider his interests, and by stressing service show him how the product will solve his problems or bring him profit and enjoyment.

Could you step out to some other firm and get a job paying twice your present salary?

You must see it. You must lift it, write on it, and operate it to learn how practical and convenient it really is and to understand what it will do for you.

It shows a method which cuts the cost of your billing to a minimum—often right in half.

With the Electrolux, you have quick-freezing ice cubes, always. It is absolutely, permanently silent. And it costs less to operate than any other refrigerator.

You have but to say the word, and our representative will gladly show you how the economies made possible by this new Remington may be brought to your own accounting.

b. Adapt the language, ideas, style, and tone of the letter to the reader. Adjust the display, the structure, and the appeal to the reader also.

These pictures show at a glance a new sort of protection for records—a protection which stops the costly losses that often wipe out your margin of profit.

Its three special ingredients cool and soothe your face from the moment you put on the lather.

Every day, year after year, Kitchen-Aid will sail through the countless tiring operations of food preparation all at the snap of a switch.

We will supply this material to you free of charge, with your firm name and address imprinted on every copy. These mailing pieces will uncover many valuable leads and pave the way for worthwhile calls.

c. Visualize the reader and take a sympathetic view of his tastes, desires, and needs. Know something about his age, sex, occupation, personality, habits, and racial and geographical environment. Try to see the reader

in his surroundings, and express your message in terms of his experience.

Conciseness

40a. State the message as briefly as possible, but at the same time clearly, completely, correctly, and courteously. Think out the letter, plan the paragraphs, and approach the central thought directly.

Not concise:

Gentlemen:

Replying to your letter of October 12, it is not customary for us to take back goods that have been purchased by dealers and carried in their stock, for, as a rule, goods that have been shipped to the dealers, unpacked, then repacked and returned to this office are not in a condition to place in our stock. Certainly the goods shown on the list enclosed with your letter would show signs of shopwear and many of the goods would be absolutely valueless, and under the circumstances we would not offer you any credit for the goods but would suggest that you sell them for whatever you can get as it is the only way that you can realize anything on them.

If we had some means of disposing of secondhand or shopworn goods, we would, of course, be pleased to make you an offer for the goods you wish to return. Unfortunately, however, our demand is entirely for new and strictly modern goods.

Very truly yours,[3]

Concise:

Gentlemen:

We wish that we could accept the merchandise which you would like to close out of your stock, as suggested in your letter of October 12. If we knew of outlets for these

[3] *Ibid.*

goods, we would be glad to dispose of them for you. Even though they are but slightly shopworn, you will appreciate the fact that they cannot be sold as new and consequently would be valueless for our distribution.

Please remember that we always try to coöperate with our dealers. In this particular case we believe that you will understand our position.

Very truly yours,[4]

b. Avoid wordiness.

Wordy: Four years ago your son left the protecting arms of grammar school for an institution of higher learning, high school. Now he has completed, or rather will have completed, his course in that never-to-be-forgotten branch of knowledge in June, two short months off.

Compact: Four years ago your son left grammar school for high school. In June he will have completed his course at Jefferson High.

c. Never omit essential ideas or words. Do not sacrifice clearness or correctness for mere brevity, or allow the letter to become curt. Avoid the telegraphic omission of pronouns, articles, or other qualifying words necessary for grammatical correctness.

Wrong: Order received and will ship on tenth.

Right: We shall ship the desk via the Illinois Central Railroad on the tenth of June, as you requested.

Wrong: Appreciate your kind inquiry about Suregrips. Would advise models still in stock. Reduction in price.

Right: Thank you for your inquiry about Suregrips. The brown oxfords in which you are interested may be purchased at Lever Brothers in your city. The price is now seven dollars.

[4] *Ibid.*

d. Mechanical helps for conciseness.

(1) Reduce predication by avoiding unnecessary verbs.

Wordy: That is what we want you to do. Win your matches by having complete confidence in your clubs. We now have in stock a new line of golf clubs. These clubs are made of the finest metal that can be procured. They are alive.

Concise: Win your matches through complete confidence in your clubs. We now have in stock a new line of LIVE clubs made of the finest metal obtainable.

Wordy: Undoubtedly you have been confronted with this question which has been important to all housewives since sour milk hot cakes went out of style.

Concise: Undoubtedly you have been confronted with this question, important to housewives since sour milk hot cakes went out of style.

(2) Do not pile up a series of adjectives before or after a noun, or a series of adverbs before or after a verb.

Wordy: An old, broken-down, dilapidated, mud-spattered automobile was limping along the highway.

Better: An old, mud-spattered automobile was limping along the highway.

Wordy: This astounding, astonishing, unbeatable bargain is available until January 15.

Better: This astonishing bargain is available until January 15.

(3) Condense a clause or a phrase into a single forceful word.

Wordy: We try to employ substitutes who are capable of filling the positions of our regular employees.

Better: We try to employ substitutes capable of filling the positions of our regular employees.

Wordy: It will bring you a portfolio of business forms that are made use of by others in the shoe business.

Better: It will bring you a portfolio of business forms used by others in the shoe business.

(4) **When futurity is not intended, make a direct assertion instead of using *WILL* and *WOULD*.**

Wordy: The new driver will often make mistakes.

Better: The new driver often makes mistakes.

Wordy: Its speed, its ease of operation, and its automatic features would make for economy.

Better: Its speed, its ease of operation, and its automatic features make for economy.

(5) **Omit *which* and *that* when they are not needed for the clearness and accuracy of the sentence.**

Public acceptance of the line you handle is the bread and butter of your business.

We know you are coming into our business with the intention of making it your life work.

Regardless of the fuel you now use in your new building, you can handle your heating plant more economically through the Honeywell control.

There is no more appropriate article you can offer your customers than a Big Ben clock.

Concreteness

41. Use words and phrases that are specific and concrete. Call up definite pictures and sensations in the reader's mind by using details that appeal to the senses.

[41]

QUALITIES

Vague: Can you drive in security knowing that your car is sturdily built?

Specific: Can you sweep over the road at 80-plus with that feeling of absolute security imparted by the Torque Tube Drive and an extra-rugged, finely balanced chassis?

Vague: Lubricants for iron and steel must give service under all conditions.

Specific: Under many-ton bearing pressures, blistering heat, and heavy shocks, lubricants for the iron and steel industry must stand up.

Vague: Housework is easy with a Vermont.

Specific: When you buy a Vermont, you buy happy afternoons.

Concrete:

Sight: Warm, friendly reds and yellows, cool greens, brilliant blues—a whole rainbow of colors for you in these Hygrade lamp bulbs.

Your veranda opens upon a glorious profusion of red roses, upon green hills with their balsam of evergreen fir and pine, upon an inspiring panorama of misty hills and snow-clad mountains.

Look again at the Royal Portable Typewriter. Observe its softly glowing Duotone and gleaming nickel.

Taste: Light, fluffy rice, invigorating broth, snow-white celery, fresh herbs, and seasonings complete a Chicken Soup that is sheer enjoyment.

Crisp, crunchy, golden-brown flakes. Each one chock-full of wonderful flavor.

The tonic juices and luscious "meat" of red-ripe tomatoes strained to a smooth puree and blended with golden creamery butter by the most famous French chefs in the world—Campbell's. Just taste it!

Touch: Outside, December is crisp and cold. Inside this blue-and-white coach are warmth and good cheer. Clean, warm air flows from Tropic-Aire heaters. Deep-cushioned individual chairs recline to any desired angle for complete relaxation.

The big, shaggy flakes burn slow, steady, and cool—hence no harshness or bite.

Within an amazingly short time, you'll find that this gentle care makes your hands softly smooth and white—charmingly young—no matter how hard you use them at household tasks or active sports.

Sound: The new Big Ben has two voices. His first morning call breaks softly into your dreams with a gentle chime, without sharp or sudden jar to your nerves.

Across the room, you won't hear it. Running as fast as your fingers can drive it, the Remington Noiseless barely whispers.

Smell: Sounds funny—maybe—to buy soap with your nose. But millions of women do. They smell the big golden bar—smell the generous amount of naphtha in it—and realize Fels-Naphtha offers not one helper, but two.

The old-fashioned buckwheats of your childhood! Remember them? Fragrant, tangy cakes, the batter mixed up at the first cold snap!

Character or Personality

42a. Express your thoughts in your own natural way. Make the letter individual, distinctive, a reflection of the attractive qualities of your own personality. Write simply, sincerely, clearly, and correctly.

b. Show confidence, enthusiasm, and cordiality. Make the letter optimistic, but courteous and dignified. Forget yourself and concentrate upon benefiting the reader.

c. **Instead of copying or imitating another writer, solve the problem in your own personal, original way.**

d. **Stereotyped language, pose, and affectation stifle character. Character excludes egotism and exaggeration. It never allows bad humor to creep into the letter, never uses mere smartness or mere cleverness, and is never guilty of misplaced humor. Character does not imply an eccentric or artificial style.**

Stereotyped: Your letter of the 15th inst. has been received and contents duly noted. The matters referred to have been given our careful attention.

"Clever": Of course, we know that when you get this information, you will be so "hot and bothered" that you will dash right over to the Western "Onion" and tell us all about it.

Eccentric: Words cannot describe this remarkable masterpiece.

Frank
daring
powerful
shameless
gripping
yes, all of this
AND MUCH MORE.

Cheerfulness

43a. **A cheerful letter is positive and constructive. Looking at the bright side of the problem, it presents the pleasing elements. It displays a spirit of optimism, good will, and service, and considers the reader's point of view in a warm, human, simple manner.**

We know you want to pay the enclosed bill promptly—that you like to keep small bills off your desk and out of your morning's mail.

It's the little things in life that count and these are the very things we so often neglect.

Being human, we can appreciate what hard work it is—and we mean just that—for most of us to sit down and write a letter. Also, we can understand how easily payment of a small bill can be unintentionally overlooked.

b. A cheerful letter eliminates negative ideas and unpleasant suggestions.

Negative: We cannot understand your attitude about this bill.

Unpleasant: How often have you come in all wet and tired from washing all morning to find the kitchen fire out and the morning's dirty dishes still in the sink?

c. Coldness, formality, and stereotyped language never produce cheerfulness.

Impersonal: Receipt is acknowledged of the above subject, part of which you sent in for adjustment as covered by your letter of February 5.

Cold: We cannot accept your order No. 4536. Requests for material are more numerous than we are able to meet, and we are supplying only those old customers who have been buying from us for some time.

Stereotyped: We are in receipt of your valued order of September 1. We beg to state that same will be shipped on September 6.

d. Avoid blunt, brusque statements and a superior, condescending attitude. Never lose patience or criticize.

Blunt: We feel that ordinary business courtesy and honesty would suggest a reply to our letters at least.

Condescending: These suits were tailored in our London shop; consequently they carry with them that swaggering English style which is impossible for our American clothes makers even to imitate.

Loss of patience: Just a glance at our bill is enough to reveal the fact that we grant cash discount only when payment is made within thirty days after the bill is rendered.

Criticism: We are surprised that you misunderstood our letter of the tenth. We surely tried to make matters clear.

e. When using cheerful phrases, use them sincerely.

Will you let us know if either of these situations may be the cause of the delay? We want to serve you in a way that is pleasing and cheerful, and naturally, shall appreciate your coöperation, too.

It has been a pleasure for us to serve you through the deferred payment account which you have recently completed.

We hope that our dealings will develop into a permanent friendship that will prove pleasant and highly satisfactory to you.

Courtesy

44a. A letter is courteous if it considers the reader's feelings and takes a sympathetic view of his problems. The courteous letter reflects the service viewpoint, the spirit of helpfulness, and acknowledges the reader's honesty and fairmindedness. It adapts its ideas, tone, and style to the reader.

We are quite sure that you do not intend to disregard our request and that your failure either to reply or to remit can be attributed to the fact that you are now busy with your Christmas trade.

Won't you go to your bookkeeper and say, "Send a check to N. M. Smollet and Company today"? Thank you.

We are glad you notified us promptly that some of your sheets were damaged in transit. It gives us a chance to clear up the difficulty without delay.

b. The courteous letter says what is most fitting in any circumstance. It avoids any idea or suggestion that might offend.

It is evident that you are not quite clear as to the matter of cash discount, which is allowed on bills paid after the invoice is rendered. Since your payment is 15 days overdue, we have passed the $675 to your credit leaving a balance of $75, the amount deducted as discount. We feel sure, however, that you now will gladly send us your check for this balance.

Unfortunately there seems to be little more that we can suggest by letter, since we have never received a report of similar trouble. We hope that you can work with as little inconvenience as possible until our representative, Mr. Mason, arrives and that you will let us know if his call does not remedy the trouble.

c. A letter is discourteous if it is sarcastic, angry, or mandatory. Statements that are blunt, brusque, or critical are never courteous. A superior, condescending air violates the spirit of courtesy.

Discourteous: Your check, received this morning, is now 15 days past due. For this reason you have no right to the $75 deducted as discount. We have credited your account for the $675 remitted and ask that you immediately send us $75 to close the account.

Discourteous: With reference to your letter of May 11 in regard to the difficulty which you have had with our merchandise recently, we are sorry that our letter of May 4 did not meet with your approval, but even though you do not agree with us, we must call your attention to one thing. If the difficulty you complain of was caused by a faulty manufacture, it would certainly seem that we would get complaints from other users. These goods are in common use and if anything is wrong, people are not at all backward about expressing themselves.

Discourteous: Was it a mistake to invest in your integrity?

d. Courtesy does not mean a humble, servile attitude. Nor does it mean insincere flattery.

Poor: We are mighty sorry this happened, and in the future we shall do everything in our power to see that things are just as you want them. Again, we are sorry.

Poor: We are very sorry to have to offend you by calling your attention to the balance on your charge account.

QUALITIES

Tone

45. Tone is an expression of the writer's mental and emotional attitudes toward his reader. It may produce in the reader mental or emotional attitudes of agreement or antagonism, acceptance or rejection, pleasure or disgust, admiration or hostility, persuasion or doubt.

a. Positive tone. A positive tone pleases the reader and conditions him for a favorable reception of the message. It is considerate, courteous, tactful, and cheerful. Its ideas and manner of statement are so chosen as to produce an effective meeting of minds of writer and reader.

Thank you for your request for samples of our Remcraft folder. We are asking a representative of our branch office to give you some samples of Remcraft so that you can test them in your own office. When he delivers these samples, our representative will welcome an opportunity to offer suggestions on any of your filing problems.

The information received through your references and your financial statement is altogether satisfactory. We are glad to open an account for you with a credit limit of $500, two per cent ten days, net thirty.

We know you want to pay the enclosed bill promptly—that you like to keep small bills off your desk and out of your morning's mail.

Here's a wonderful new-fashioned fruit cake. Try it on your family! Make it just as the recipe directs, and you'll have as perfect a holiday cake as you've ever dreamed of making.

b. Negative tone. A negative tone displeases or irritates the reader. It produces doubt, indifference, hostility, or rejection and thus makes difficult an effective meeting of minds. Misspellings, grammatical errors, rhe-

torical ineptitudes, and a suggestion of the opposite of what the writer really intends are negative.

If it isn't too much trouble, will you send me some information on the raising of sweet peas?

As per your inquiry of May 8, we are sending you the booklet you requested.

From what I know of your present financial condition, I must say that you are in a bad situation.

Don't say *No.* This is a wonderful bargain.

I wish to get employment during the summer vacation. An interview would benefit both of us.

Inquiries, Answers, Orders

Sales Inquiries

46a. Sales inquiries are concerned with catalogues, booklets, pamphlets, prices, information about service, descriptions of products, and similar matters. The letter should be brief and simple.

Gentlemen:

Please send me your booklet "Radiant Heating in the Modern Home," as advertised in the June number of *The American Builder*.

Very truly yours,

b. Sales inquiries should be clear and concise, definite and courteous.

Gentlemen:

Please quote me your f.o.b. Detroit price on your economy model six-cylinder, two-ton trucks with hydraulic hoists and dump bodies.

Very truly yours,

c. In seeking detailed information or asking definite questions, an arrangement of the points in tabulated form will help to make the inquiry clear and will help the reader to give satisfactory information.

Gentlemen:

I have just read your advertisement in the June issue of *Good Housekeeping* and am considering the advisability of taking your commercial course. Before deciding, I should like a little more information.

1. Does the course include English grammar?
2. How long would it take me to complete the course?
3. If I devote all my time to my course, can I finish in six months?
4. Would it be possible for me to secure a position within twenty miles of Cedar Rapids upon the completion of my course?
5. Just what help do you give your students in finding positions?

Please let me hear from you at once, because I want to start as soon as possible.

Very truly yours,

d. Avoid negative suggestion—that is, any statement that suggests to the reader that the request should not be granted. Do not apologize and do not thank the reader "in advance" (an apology implies an offense, and thanking in advance may be presumptuous).

Wrong:

Gentlemen:

I am sorry to trouble you, but I should like to know the price of the green and gold desk set with the onyx base. *Thanking you in advance,*

Yours truly,

Gentlemen:

If it is not too much bother, I should like to have a little information about the automatic clothes dryer advertised in *Collier's*. I am considering buying one and would like to have *all the information you think is necessary.*

Yours truly,

e. Sales inquiries may be solicited (written in answer to advertising) or unsolicited (written on the inquirer's own initiative).

Gentlemen:

Please send me full information on your Assured Retirement Income Plan advertised in the November issue of *Time.*

Very truly yours,

Gentlemen:

Please send me authentic medical information on the benefits of ultra-violet. Is the General Electric Sunlamp effective in treating chronic sinusitis?

Very truly yours,

Non-sales Inquiries

47. Non-sales inquiries request information, advice, or favors not directly related to the sale of goods. The letter contains the following points:

(1) The reason for the inquiry
(2) The question or request.
(3) The advantage to the reader in granting the request, or some other matter to induce favorable action.
(4) A statement of appreciation.

Note: The positions of the first and second headings may be reversed; in some situations, the third is omitted.

Gentlemen:

Reason: We are investigating certain conditions which we believe to exist in the teaching profession. In order that we may intelligently complete our analysis, it is necessary that we secure additional information.

Request: With this objective in mind, we have prepared a questionnaire, a copy of which is enclosed. We earnestly invite your coöperation.

A few of the questions asked may possibly appear to be so personal that you will not feel justified in answering them. Please, however, reply to as many of them as you feel free to answer, and return the questionnaire in the enclosed, stamped envelope.

Advantage: Without your personal assistance, our investigation must fail. To those who assist us, we shall in due course furnish a résumé of our findings.

Appreciation: Meanwhile we confidently anticipate an early reply, and we assure you we shall greatly appreciate your sincere coöperation in answering as many of the questions as you can.

Very truly yours,[1]

Answers

TO SALES INQUIRIES

48a. Every sales inquiry presents a sales opportunity. Do not, therefore, answer inquiries in a routine manner. Make the answer create good will. Arouse a desire for the product by a suggestive and persuasive description of it.

b. Answers to inquiries about products and services are really sales letters. Form letters and form paragraphs incorporating sales principles are usually written in advance to handle inquiries resulting from advertising.

c. Make answers to sales inquiries helpful and considerate, and show a desire to serve.

[1] From A. C. Babenroth, *Modern Business English.* New York: Prentice-Hall, Inc.

d. Make answers to sales inquiries clear, courteous, and complete.

Dear Miss Bell:

As you requested in your letter of October 25, we enclose a folder describing the complete line of Underwood Portable Typewriters.

Underwood, typewriter leader of the world, offers a portable for every purse and purpose. When your homework, social correspondence, club notes, and letters are written the Underwood way, you will find that your Underwood becomes one of your most priceless possessions.

The ease, speed, and legibility with which your thoughts are transferred to paper the Underwood way provide a two-way benefit by making both writing and reading a pleasure. Your personal typewriter will give you more golden hours of leisure time.

The Underwood dealer in your neighborhood will be glad to demonstrate any of our models. May I suggest that you call on him soon in order to learn the many advantages of owning your own personal Underwood Portable Typewriter?

Very truly yours,

UNDERWOOD CORPORATION

TO NON-SALES INQUIRIES

48e. In granting requests, cheerfully give the information requested, or grant the favor. You may offer further assistance. The letter, if possible, closes with sales material.

Dear Mr. Grant:

Your letter, addressed to the International General Electric Company in New York, has been sent here to Schenectady, the headquarters of our publicity department.

We shall be glad to coöperate with you in whatever way we can in your broadcast featuring important scientific developments for "The World Tomorrow." We are enclosing several publications which tell in brief some of the latest developments in the electrical field. If any of this material will lend itself to your series of broadcasts, we shall be glad to send you more detailed information on request.

We hope this material will reach you in time to be of help in planning your program. If General Electric can be of further assistance in this project, please do not hesitate to write.

Very truly yours,

GENERAL ELECTRIC COMPANY

f. **In refusing requests, make the letter courteous and concise.** State the reasons for the refusal, refuse the request, and express regret. The letter may open with the refusal, the reasons, or a courteous explanation. It may close with a sales talk about the product, an effort to sell the reader the refusal, or an offer of other information or assistance.

Dear Miss Ronson:

Because each woman's search for youth and beauty is an individual problem, it necessarily requires individual attention.

We, therefore, do not find the use of set formulas suitable to the requirements of our customers. We are sorry that we do not have any of the booklets you requested us to send you.

Why not see your nearest Dorothy Dale representative for a personal analysis of your beauty problems, and be sure that you are using the course of treatment exactly suited to your type of beauty?

Very truly yours,

DOROTHY DALE, INC.

Order Letters

49a. When no order blank is available, the order letter contains the following elements:

[49]

(1) **A complete and exact description of the goods.** Give the catalogue number and the trade name of the goods and their quantity, size, color, style, and price.

(2) **Shipping directions.** Give the complete address, the shipping date, and the manner of shipment.

(3) **The manner of payment.** State whether payment is to be made by account, money order, check, draft, or C.O.D.

(4) **Special considerations.** Include any special information that will help the seller to give you satisfaction. The close may stress such points as price, discounts, quality, and date of shipment.

Gentlemen:

Send me at once the following articles, listed in your spring catalogue, and charge them to my account:

Qty.	Article	Price	Amount
3	doz. No. 432 Men's Cotton Hose, Black only, asstd. sizes	@$ 2.25	$ 6.75
5	doz. No. 285 Women's Silk Stockings, Black, asstd. sizes	@$ 9.50	$47.50
11	doz. No. 113 Children's Tan School Stockings, asstd. sizes	@$ 2.40	$26.40
20	doz. No. 440 Men's Initial Handkerchiefs	@$ 1.00	$20.00
1	doz. No. 236 Silkoline Umbrellas, 26-inch	@$16.00	$16.00
2	doz. No. 82 Men's Work Shirts, asstd. sizes	@$ 8.40	$16.80
	Total		$133.45

Ship all these goods by freight, except the children's stockings, which you may send by express, collect, as I need them right away.

Very truly yours,

b. Indent the items of the order and place each item on a separate line.

c. Give the price of each item and also the total price.

d. When money is enclosed, state clearly the amount and in what form it is.

e. Do not write out numbers in order letters. Use figures.

f. First orders requesting credit may contain references or a financial statement.

Routine Acknowledgments

50. For routine acknowledgments of orders, most firms use printed forms and fill-ins. Both post cards and letter-forms are used.

Thank you for your order No.________of________. We shall ship the goods by________within________days.

We appreciate your patronage and shall endeavor to render you every service possible.

Individual Acknowledgments

51a. Individual personal letters are written to acknowledge first orders from new customers, unusually large orders from old customers, defective orders, orders requiring substitution, and orders that must be refused, and to handle irregular or unusual situations.

Dear Mrs. Jacobs:

Your order recently placed with us for a refrigerator is greatly appreciated. The delivery has been arranged to conform with your wishes, and we sincerely hope that the refrigerator and our services are satisfactory to you in every respect.

A copy of your order enclosed indicates the terms of your account. Please communicate with us at once if the terms of this agreement are not according to your understanding with our representative.

We invite you to share the remarkable savings now possible on every type of home furnishing at Barker Bros. From our very complete stocks there is a continuous succession of feature values, representing the lowest prices in fifteen years. A schedule of payments for additional purchases may easily be arranged to conform with your budget.

It is our hope that this is only the beginning of a very pleasant and permanent friendship.

Yours very truly,

BARKER BROS. INC.

b. Acknowledge orders immediately.

Dear Mr. Jones:

We wish to acknowledge and thank you for the order which was recently placed with our branch office.

For your convenience in making payments promptly, we are enclosing a book of Installment Payment Coupons, which is self-explanatory. To each coupon is attached a return envelope for each monthly payment. It is important that a coupon be sent to us with each payment.

If the detail contained in this book does not agree with your records, will you please inform us to that effect?

When writing us in regard to this contract, please quote your account number.

Very truly yours,

UNDERWOOD CORPORATION

c. The content and plan of the acknowledgment depend upon the particular order. Acknowledgments ordinarily cover the following points:

(1) **The expression of appreciation for the order.**

(2) **References to the date of the order, the number of the order, and the method of payment. The order may be restated.**

(3) **Shipping information.** If the order has been filled and forwarded, give the date of shipment and the method. If the order has not been filled, explain the reason and suggest some adjustment of the difficulty.

(4) **A short sales talk** inducing confidence in the house, its goods and service; the indication of a desire to serve; and an invitation to future orders. In letters to dealers, an offer may be made of such dealer-service helps as advertising—national or sectional, partial payment for local advertising, copy and cuts for local advertising; form letters covering a list of the dealer's prospects; aids in window display; folders and booklets; samples; canvassers and demonstrators.

New Customers

Gentlemen:

Appreciation: Your order of September 1 came in today, and we thank you for it.

Restatement: The 500 sheets of 20 gauge, 12 by 96, will be shipped on September 6 over the Big Four.

Shipping information: We have taken every precaution to see that this material is well crated and accurately marked so that it may reach you promptly. Please notify us if it does not arrive on time and in the best of condition.

[51]

Sales material: It is indeed gratifying to us, and I know it must be to you, to learn that your business prospects are becoming brighter from day to day. There can be no question that a quality product, such as you are placing upon the market, will find a growing demand.

We want you to feel that, as manufacturers of your sheet metal, we shall be glad to help you in any way possible.

Very truly yours,[2]

Old Customers

Dear Mr. Burge:

Thank you for your generous order of June 8, which we take as an indication of your increased business in our goods.

3 Frocks of Fashion, No. 208, Size 34	@ $39.00	$117.00
2 Ultra Smart, No. 214, Size 34	@ $35.00	$ 70.00
4 Utility, No. 126, Size 38	@ $19.00	$ 76.00
6 French Inspiration, No. 38, Size 34	@ $49.00	$294.00
Total		$557.00

These gowns are being shipped today by United States Railway Express and should reach you on Thursday in time for the week-end trade.

Your customers will find in these smart models just the quality and design most in vogue among women who pride themselves on their dress. As in the past, we are supplying the unusual, the different, the uncommon modes at lowest prices. To sell our gowns is to convince your fashionable trade that you have initiative

[2] From *Making Letters Talk Business*, The American Rolling Mill Co.

and that you are the one who first features new styles for those who look for inspiration and individuality in dress.

The styles we are sending you are authentic, original, and appropriate.

The most critical buyers will immediately recognize the quality and style of these gowns.

We assure you of our personal attention and of our steadfast desire to please you.

Very truly yours,[3]

Defective Orders

52. When the customer's order is indefinite or incomplete, the acknowledgment tactfully requests additional information. It never blames the customer. The letter may contain:

a. Thanks for the order.

b. A courteous request for additional information.

c. An attempt to "sell" the request by showing that it is made with the customer's interests in view and that the firm desires to give efficient and prompt service.

Dear Mr. Hurley:

Thank you for your order of April 18.

We are sorry that we are unable to ship your goods without further information.

Please give us the catalogue number, the size, and the price of the shoes you ordered.

Do you wish them sent by parcel post?

We are holding your check until we hear from you.

[3] From A. C. Babenroth, *Modern Business English.* New York: Prentice-Hall, Inc.

If you will please fill out the enclosed blank and mail it at once in the enclosed stamped envelope, we shall forward the order promptly and to your complete satisfaction.

Very truly yours,

Delayed or Incomplete Shipments

53. When the shipment has been delayed or is incomplete, the letter explains what has been done with the order, expresses regret, and may offer an adjustment.

Gentlemen:

Your order No. 245 was billed out this morning over the Southern Pacific Railroad. I am very sorry that there was a delay, but this was unavoidable because of a shortage of the quality of coal we know your trade requires.

Ever since the recent labor troubles, we have had a little difficulty in keeping supplied with this grade. We could, however, have made prompt shipment of an inferior grade, but as I know that your customers demand the best, I waited until I had coal of the quality I usually ship you.

I hope this supply reaches you before your present stock is exhausted.

Very truly yours,

Out of Stock

54. When the goods are out of stock, send a personally dictated letter. It should:

a. Express thanks for the order and regret that the order cannot be filled as the customer desired;

b. Explain that the predicament is unusual and is not likely to recur; and

c. Ask permission to make a substitution, using a sales talk to induce acceptance, or inform the customer that a substitution has been made and

tell him that the goods may be returned if he is not satisfied. If no substitution can be made, the letter should offer any possible assistance.

Dear Madam:

Thank you for your order of May 28.

We should like to fill your order for the Fashion Blouse, A347, Size 38, but we have received more orders than we expected, with the result that our large reserve stock has been completely sold out.

The manufacturer is no longer able to supply this blouse, but we fortunately have in stock a blouse of the same high quality and exquisite style, at a slightly lower price. You will find this waist listed and illustrated in our catalogue, on page 15, A348. We can send you the waist promptly if we receive your order within a few days. This very popular model is now selling as fast as the model you ordered.

Remember you are fully protected by our guarantee, "Money cheerfully and promptly refunded if you are not satisfied." We are certain, however, that you will not part with the blouse when you see it.

Just write the catalogue number of the blouse and the size you desire on the enclosed special order blank, and mail it to us in the enclosed stamped envelope.

The blouse will reach you promptly if you do not delay.

Very truly yours,[4]

Refusals of Orders

55. When an order must be refused, write a personal, sincere letter that will build good will and leave open the way for future business. The refusal letter may contain:

a. An expression of appreciation for the order.

[4] *Ibid.*

[55]

b. A courteous, definite explanation of the facts.

c. An attempt to "sell" the refusal, showing the customer that the refusal is in his own interests.

Dear Miss Boyce:

Appreciation: We appreciate very much your order and remittance.

Explanation: One of the ingredients used in the manufacture of Studio Girl Radiant Lustre and Studio Girl Hair Conditioner is needed in the treatment of our injured boys. For that reason, we have discontinued manufacturing both of these fine products until there is more than enough of this precious ingredient for their use—plus a surplus for us.

Action taken: We are, therefore, returning your remittance with our thanks and our regrets; but we are keeping your name prominently before us and will notify you by mail just as soon as these two products can be supplied.

Sales material: Meanwhile, we hope you will continue to be a regular Studio Girl Shampoo user. If you enjoy using Studio Girl, we hope you will mention your discovery to your friends.

We also would like to extend to you a cordial invitation to visit our offices on your next trip to Hollywood. It would be a sincere pleasure to contribute to the joy of your visit in any way we can.

Very truly yours,

STUDIO GIRL SHAMPOO

Remittances

56. Acknowledge remittances immediately and thank the customer.

Gentlemen:

Thank you for your check in payment of your May account.

We wish to express our appreciation of the satisfactory manner in which you have made your payments.

Very truly yours,

Gentlemen:

Payment in full for your vacuum sweeper has been received. Thank you.

We hope that you have found your DeLuxe satisfactory in every way and that it is giving you all the service that you desire.

Very truly yours,

Credit Letters

Credit Information

57a. The credit letter is a selling letter; it sells not only the important privilege of buying on future payment, but also good will and business coöperation. Whether the credit application is accepted or refused, the credit letter should be considerate, helpful, and tactful.

b. Credit is the firm's faith in the customer's ability and willingness to pay at a specified time in the future for goods purchased now. It represents the customer's power to buy without paying cash. (For variant definitions see any of the standard texts on credit.)

c. Information about the credit applicant may be secured from him and from other sources.

DIRECT SOURCES

(1) **Personal interviews with the credit applicant.**

(2) **Financial statements submitted by the credit applicant** (balance sheets and profit and loss statements secured directly from the credit applicant or through mercantile credit agency reports). **Credit application forms supplied by the firm and filled out by the applicant** (standard forms are furnished members by local and national retail credit associations).

INDIRECT SOURCES

(1) **Other creditors of the applicant** (through a credit interchange bureau or directly through other creditors).

(2) **Retail credit bureaus.** Local bureaus exist in nearly all cities; they are affiliated nationally through the National Retail Credit Men's Association and its Credit Interchange Bureaus and coördinated through the National Consumer Credit Reporting Corporation. Associated Credit Bureaus of America are the affiliated bureaus of the National Retail Credit Association.

(3) **General or special mercantile agencies.** These supply capital and credit ratings and complete special reports on individual concerns. The general mercantile agency is Dun & Bradstreet, Inc. Special mercantile agencies cover only a special line of business or a restricted area; for example, Credit Interchange Bureau System of the National Association of Credit Men; Special Industries Division, Dun & Bradstreet, Inc.; The National Credit Office, Inc.; The Credit Clearing House, Inc. There are also special agencies for various lines of trade.

(4) **Credit applicant's references.** The main value of personal references is in tracing skips or applicants of unsatisfactory standing.

(5) **Banks in which the credit applicant has an account.** Information from banks varies in kind and detail. Banks often will give no information about savings accounts; in reference to checking accounts, some banks will indicate the approximate size of the account, loans outstanding, and an opinion of the applicant.

(6) **Attorneys.** Because they often function legally in collection cases, attorneys may supply useful supplementary information; they may also supply information as to the applicant's reputation, local business conditions, property valuation, and the value of the applicant's business.

CREDIT LETTERS

SOURCES OF MERCANTILE CREDIT INFORMATION RELATING TO BUSINESS ACTIVITY

(1) **Bank reports.** *Federal Reserve Bulletin. The National City Bank Bulletin. The Guaranty Bulletin. The Cleveland Trust Letter.*

(2) **United States Government reports.** The Department of Agriculture: *The Agricultural Situation* and *Crop Estimates.* The Department of Commerce: current data for many kinds of business activity; reports of the Market Research Division; *Domestic Commerce* and *The Survey of Current Business.* The Department of Labor: *Labor Information Bulletin; The Monthly Labor Review; Annual Report of the Secretary of Labor.*

(3) **Business and financial reporting agencies.** *Moody's Investors Service. Standard Daily Trade Service. Brookmire Economic Service. Babson's Business Report Service. American Institute of Finance. Dun & Bradstreet, Inc.* Financial news journals, such as *Wall Street Journal, Journal of Commerce, Commercial and Financial Chronicle.*

(4) **Trade association journals.** Monthly journals of the particular trade associations. National Association of Credit Men, *Credit and Financial Management.* National Retail Credit Association, *The Credit World.*

Elements of Credit

58a. An examination of the following factors determines whether the credit application is accepted or refused:

(1) **Capital.** Capital is the financial strength of the risk or the means of production at his disposal. The credit man analyzes property and financial statements of the risk to discover the ratio be-

tween his assets and his liabilities and the amount of his assets readily convertible into cash. The risk's working capital, that is, the difference between his current assets and current liabilities, represents his debt-paying power. In the case of an individual rather than of a business concern, the credit man considers the risk's income, earning power, investments, real estate holdings, property such as automobiles, life insurance, financial obligations, expenses, expenditures, mortgages, bank loans, and other indebtedness.

(2) **Capacity.** Capacity is the individual's ability for doing business and his ability to pay; it is his ability to use effectively the income-producing means at his disposal in such a way as to assure the creditor payment of his debts; it is based upon the relation between the risk's income and his financial obligations and expenses. It may be judged by an analysis of the kind and volume of his business, the location of his business, and his personal aptitude for business. It may be judged by the efficiency with which he conducts his business, his technical ability, ambition, alertness, shrewdness, buying and selling methods, policies, and general business management. In the case of an employee, it may be judged by the consistency with which he holds his position, his record of advancement, and his general competence.

(3) **Character.** The applicant's character may be determined by examining his known paying habits and his present and past reputation for honesty, fair dealing, moral conduct, good personal habits, and uprightness.

(4) **Conditions.** Economic and social conditions (seasonal or cyclical and those peculiar to a partic-

ular area or trade) may affect capital, capacity, and character favorably or adversely. Sometimes, conditions change the income potentialities of individuals by affecting their trade, job, or line of business.

b. In his investigation of the above factors, the credit manager wants to know if the credit applicant is able to pay, if he is willing to pay, if he can be relied upon to pay at the specified time, and if he fails to pay whether he can be forced to pay. Capital and capacity are the bases of ability to pay; willingness is dependent upon character. But conditions may affect all three adversely or favorably.

c. For retail charge accounts, a financial limit, which is somewhat flexible, is set for each account. Terms of payment at a specified date are stated, usually in full by the tenth of the following month.

The credit limit is ascertained in reference to the applicant's monthly income and his fixed financial obligations. In determining the risk's debt-paying ability, the credit man considers the proportion of income the applicant is likely to spend monthly on the type of merchandise sold by the firm and his known charge accounts with stores carrying similar merchandise. Information secured from local retail credit bureaus is often used in determining the credit limit; this information is supplied to the bureau by other creditor firms.

d. Installment credit limits are usually much larger than the limit of an individual's monthly charge account, because each payment is relatively small, the full payment is spread over a comparatively long period, and the creditor has the legal right of repossession.

Replies to Credit Applications

59a. When an applicant sends a letter requesting credit, a request with an order, or merely an order without cash remittance, the firm's reply usually takes the following form:

Opening: The applicant is welcomed and thanked for his request or order.

Explanation: The firm's procedure or policy in credit matters is explained.

Request: The applicant is asked for credit information and credit references. Usually, a printed form is enclosed for the applicant to fill out.

Close: Prompt action is stimulated by showing the customer that it is to his interest to reply at once.

Gentlemen:

Opening: Thank you for your order of the tenth placed with Mr. Jones. It calls for a well-selected merchandise assortment, for which you will find ready and profitable sale.

Request: In connection with the usual credit formalities of a new account, our Credit Department would appreciate your filling out and returning the enclosed property statement blank.

Explanation: This is not more than any conservative house requires, and we feel that you will appreciate our coming directly and frankly to you for such information. This information is for our own credit files only, where it will be treated in confidence.

Close: Your account can be formally opened just as soon as this information reaches us, when shipment will be rushed.

It is our hope that this is but the beginning of a long business relationship that we shall try hard to make both pleasing and profitable for you.

Very truly yours,[1]

Dear Mr. Wilson:

Opening: The order you recently placed with Mr. Marshall, our representative, is sincerely appreciated. We hope that within the next few days we may be able actively to begin a mutually pleasant and profitable business friendship.

This order amounts to approximately $158. It includes a wide range of items which should find a ready sale in your city.

Explanation: You realize, of course, that this is our first business contact with you. It is our policy, during the initial period of our dealings with new accounts, to ask that the first order be handled along prescribed lines. This is in no way a reflection on the customer's standing, nor is it indicative of any reluctance on our part to extend the usual courtesy of a credit understanding.

Request: This policy places us under the obligation of asking our new friends to pay for at least one-third of the first order on a cash basis, pending the establishment of an open account. We have found this arrangement to be satisfactory not only from our point of view but also from that of the dealers who contemplate handling our goods. It saves

[1] From *Postage and the Mailbag.*

time and prevents loss of sales during the usual preliminary negotiations.

Close: I am confident that you will appreciate the fairness and reasonableness of our position and that you will be willing to coöperate as indicated, thereby enabling us to make prompt shipment of this order.

If you will send us your check for $50, addressed for my personal attention, I shall arrange to have this merchandise delivered to you as promptly as possible.

Very truly yours,[2]

b. The essential element of this type of letter is tact. Make the customer feel your friendly interest in him, and so phrase the request that he understands that the information requested is part of the customary routine of credit extension.

c. Specimens of a credit application form and financial statement may be found on pp. 140-142.

d. Established credit accounts are asked at certain periods to submit current financial statements. Below is a specimen letter requesting such a financial statement; the financial statement blank itself is on pp. 138-139.

Gentlemen: Attention: ____________________, Treasurer

To complete our periodical review of the credit files we maintain on all accounts, we desire to secure a copy of your most recent financial statement.

You will find that the better acquaintance between us brought about by the financial statement you send will be beneficial to yourselves as well as to us. Also, you may rest assured any information passed on to us will be treated in confidence.

[2] *Ibid.*

[59]

REPLIES TO CREDIT APPLICATIONS

For your convenience, a financial statement blank is enclosed, and your prompt attention to this request will be appreciated.

Very truly yours,

RADIO CORPORATION OF AMERICA

(front)

FINANCIAL STATEMENT

______________ (Company)

______________ (Address)

(Date Here) ______________ 19__

Gentlemen:

The undersigned ______________, merchants doing business at ______________, County of ______________, State of ______________ for the purpose of obtaining credit for goods to be sold me or us by you, or for extension granted me or us on my or our account with you hereby give you the following as a true statement of my or our assets and liabilities, and general financial condition. This may be considered a "continuing statement" and substantially correct until notice is given to you in writing by me or us of any material change in my or our financial condition.

ASSETS — (Fill all blanks, writing "no" or "none" where necessary to complete information) — LIABILITIES

ASSETS

Cash	$
Notes and Trade Acceptance	$
Accounts Receivable	$
*Merchandise	$
Total Quick Assets	$
Furniture, Fixtures and Equipment	$
Real Estate (Business)	$
Real Estate (Personal)	$
Other Assets	$
	$
Total Fixed Assets	$
Total All Assets	$

*Valued at cost? ______________ or market? ______________

What assets are pledged as collateral? ______________

LIABILITIES

Accounts Payable (Not Due)	$
Accounts Payable (Past Due)	$
Notes and Trade Acceptances:	
To Banks	$
To Trade Creditors	$
To Others	$
Total Current Liabilities	$
Liens and Chattel Mortgages on Merchandise, Furniture, Fixtures and Equipment	$
Mortgages on Real Estate (Business)	$
Mortgages on Real Estate (Personal)	$
Other Liabilities	$
Total Fixed Liabilities	$
Total All Liabilities	$
NET WORTH — If Corporation — Capital Stock — Preferred	$
NET WORTH — If Corporation — Capital Stock — Common	$
NET WORTH — If Corporation — Surplus, Earned	$
NET WORTH — If Individual or Partnership — Surplus, Unearned	$
NET WORTH — If Individual or Partnership — Capital	$
TOTAL (Liabilities and Net Worth)	$

CONTINGENT LIABILITIES — On customers' accounts sold $______ On customers' notes or trade acceptances discontinued or sold $______ All other contingent liabilities, including those as accommodation endorser, surety, guarantor, or for law suits, judgments, etc. $______ TOTAL CONTINGENT LIABILITIES $______

ACCOUNTS PAYABLE (Please give largest suppliers)

Name of Firm	Address	Total Amount Owing	Amount Past Due

Annual Sales $______ Gross Profit $______ Annual Expenses $______

Net Profit $______ Other Income $______ Insurance on Merchandise and Equipment $______

Insurance on Real Estate $______ Location and Kind of Business? ______________

______________ How long there? ______

Are books of account kept? ______ Last inventory date? ______ Do you hold any merchandise on consignment or conditional sale? What amount? ______ Is any machinery or equipment held on conditional sale or lease? Amount to be paid thereon? ______________

Bank with ______________ Address ______________

If partnership, give name of partners:
If corporation, give name of each officer:

____

____

This financial statement, both printed and written, has been carefully read by the undersigned and a full and correct statement of my or our financial condition as of the date first above written.

Firm Signature ______________

By ______________

(See other Side)

(back)

DESCRIPTION OF REAL ESTATE OWNED

In Name of	Description	Value		Mortgages	Equity
		Assessed	Cash		

THE VALUE OF A FINANCIAL STATEMENT

Practically all businesses, however large or small, find it necessary and profitable to operate at times on borrowed capital. Banks supply part of the temporary funds but much more is obtained from suppliers of merchandise who extend credit on regular terms.

Before wholesalers and manufacturers are confident that you represent certain financial strength and business ability, it is necessary for them to know something about your business. The financial statement on the reverse side will give this information. Be sure that it is made out correctly.

Good credit is an asset in your business and possession of it marks you as a good business man. The people from whom you buy know that you have both the ability and willingness to pay your bills promptly.

Your creditors are in a sense partners in your business and are vitally concerned with your business welfare.

SEAL HERE

SEAL HERE

SEAL HERE

POSTAGE STAMP HERE

[59]

APPLICATION FOR CREDIT
WITH

Form Adopted By and For Members of

THE CREDIT BUREAU
EUGENE. OREGON

TREAT YOUR CREDIT AS A SACRED TRUST

NUMBER .... DATE ....

FULL NAME (Surname First)	FULL GIVEN NAME	INITIAL	AGE	Husband or Wife's GIVEN NAME	Age

RESIDENCE		How Long
FORMER ADDRESS		How Long
BUSINESS or OCCUPATION	BY WHOM EMPLOYED / BUS. ADDRESS	How Long
FORMER BUS. or OCCUPATION	BY WHOM EMPLOYED / BUS. ADDRESS	How Long
WIFE or HUSBAND EMPLOYED AS	BY WHOM / APPROX. INCOME $ Per	How Long

OWN REAL ESTATE LOCATED AT	VALUE $	MORTGAGED TO	AMOUNT

RENT		OWNER	Monthly Rental	CHILDREN At Home	CHILDREN Employed
	FURN. APARTMENT?				
	UNFURN. APARTMENT?				
	RESIDENCE?				

NAME OF NEAREST RELATIVE (Other than husband or wife) ADDRESS

BANK (Checking) (Saving) (Name of Bank) BRANCH

LIFE INSURANCE $ Name of Insurance Co. APPROX. INCOME $ Per.

TRADE REFERENCES

FIRM or STORE	Kind of Mdse. Bought	Account Is Now Open	Account Is Now Paid-Date

List on reverse side of this application any unpaid balances on installment accounts and monthly payments thereon.

Personal References ....

The above information is for the purpose of obtaining credit, and is warranted to be true. I agree to pay all bills by the 10th of the month following purchase or as otherwise expressly agreed.

Special Terms If Any ....

SIGNATURE ....

Amount Credit	APPROVED
$	....

(front)

Form 3

Date__________________19___

FINANCIAL STATEMENT OF________________________________

At Close of Books on________________19___Address________________

Kind of Business________________City________________State________

ISSUED TO________________________________ { Name of firm asking for statement

(THIS FORM APPROVED AND PUBLISHED BY THE NATIONAL ASSOCIATION OF CREDIT MEN)

For the purpose of obtaining merchandise from you on credit, or for the extension of credit, we make the following statement in writing, intending that you should rely thereon respecting our exact financial condition on (date)________________19____

(PLEASE ANSWER ALL QUESTIONS. WHEN NO FIGURES ARE INSERTED, WRITE WORD "NONE")

ASSETS	Dollars	Cents	LIABILITIES	Dollars	Cents
Cash (Total)			**Accounts Payable for Merchandise, etc., Past Due**		
(In Bank $________)			**Accounts Payable for Merchandise, etc., not due**		
Accounts Receivable			**Acceptances and Notes Payable for Merchandise**		
(60 Days or More Past Due $________)			**Owing to Finance Companies, Banks, or Others**		
(Amt. Sold or Pledged $________)			(Secured by $______of Accounts Pledged, Assigned or Sold)		
Notes and Trade Acceptances Receivable			(Secured by $______of Notes or Acceptances Pledged or Assigned)		
(Amt. Sold or Pledged $________)			(Secured by $______of Merchandise Inventory Pledged or Assigned)		
Merchandise Inventory, Not on Consignment or Conditional Sale, at Cost or Market whichever is lower			**Notes to Banks** (without security)		
(Amount Pledged $________)			**Notes and Accounts Payable to Partners, Officers, Directors or Stockholders**		
Other Current Assets (Describe)			**Notes and Accounts Payable to Others**		
			Interest, Accrued		
			Taxes, Accrued		
			Unpaid City and/or State Sales Taxes, Accrued		
TOTAL CURRENT ASSETS			**Debt Payable in Less Than One Year** ($______ Secured by Mortgage on Land and Buildings, $______ secured by Chattel Mortgage or other Liens on________ (Property))		
Due from Affiliated or Subsidiary Concerns			**Other Current Liabilities** (describe):		
Land (see reverse side for details)					
Buildings (at depreciated cost; see reverse side)			TOTAL CURRENT LIABILITIES		
Machinery (at cost less $______depreciation)			**Debt Payable After One Year** (secured by Mortgage on Land and Buildings)		
Fixtures and Other Equipment (at cost, less $______ depreciation)			**Debt Payable After One Year** (secured by Chattel Mortgage or other Liens on________ (Property))		
Notes and Accounts Due from Partners, Officers, Directors, Stockholders or others not Customers			**Other Liabilities Not Current** (describe):		
Prepaid Expenses (insurance premiums, supplies, etc.)			TOTAL LIABILITIES		
Other Assets (describe):			NET WORTH — If Corporation: Capital Stock (Preferred)		
			NET WORTH — If Corporation: Capital Stock (Common)		
			NET WORTH — If Corporation: Surplus, Earned		
			NET WORTH — If Corporation: Surplus, Unearned		
			NET WORTH — If Individual or partnership: Capital		
TOTAL ASSETS			TOTAL LIABILITIES AND NET WORTH		

Are you a corporation, co-partnership, or individually owned?________Your terms of sale________

How long have you been established?______ If incorporated, under the laws of what state?______When?______

Contingent Liabilities on notes or trade acceptances discounted or sold (not stated above) $______ All other contingent liabilities, including those as accommodation endorser, surety, guarantor, or for law suits, judgments, etc. $______

Is it your regular practice to sell, pledge or assign your accounts?______ What amount of your accounts, notes and acceptances is sold, pledged, or assigned to banks? $______ Finance companies? $______ Others? $______

Is any part of your assets (except accounts, notes, acceptances and merchandise) assigned or pledged as security for any debt, or is there any mortgage or other lien thereon?______If so, give details of assets assigned or pledged, and details of liabilities thus secured______

______Actual date of last inventory______

Does merchandise inventory shown in the foregoing statement represent the value of physical inventory?______ If not, state basis used and date inventory was last reconciled and adjusted with stock______

What amount of merchandise do you hold on consignment or conditional sale not included in assets? $______

What amount of machinery or equipment is held under conditional sale? $______ (Balance due $______ at $______ per month)

If machinery or equipment is under lease contract, state amount of monthly payments $______

If business premises are leased, state term and annual rental______

In whose name is title to business premises?______

What books of account do you keep? (Give complete list)______

Does the foregoing statement agree with those books?______Do you keep cost records?______Are your books of account audited?______

If so, by whom?______Date of last audit______

Names and addresses of your banks______

(OVER)

[59]

(back)

IF PARTNERSHIP, NAME PARTNERS. IF CORPORATION, NAME OFFICERS: (Give residence addresses also)

DETAILS OF LAND AND BUILDINGS:

DESCRIPTION & LOCATION	TITLE IN NAME OF	Cost	Accumulated Depreciation	Depreciated Cost	Assessed Value	ENCUMBRANCES	
						Amount	To Whom

If land, buildings, machinery, fixtures and other equipment are valued on basis other than cost, explain such basis

INSURANCE PROTECTION CARRIED

Merchandise (Fire) $ Buildings (Fire) $ Furniture, Equipment (Fire) $
Employers' Liability $ Fidelity Bonds $ Burglary $
Life Insurance for Benefit of Business $ Credit Insurance $
Have You Had a Recent Insurance Analysis Made by a Competent Insurance Agent?
Name of Agent Making Analysis Address
Is Any Insurance Assigned? If So, To Whom?

BUY PRINCIPALLY FROM THE FOLLOWING FIRMS:

NAME	ADDRESS	AMOUNT OWING	
		Open Account	Notes, etc.

SUMMARY STATEMENT OF PROFIT AND LOSS FOR YEAR ENDED

Sales (net)		Gross Profit on Sales		Net Profit on Sales	
Deduct: Cost of Goods Sold		Deduct: Expenses		Add: Other Income	
GROSS PROFIT ON SALES		NET PROFIT ON SALES		NET INCOME	

AMOUNT OF ANNUAL SALES FOR CASH $ AMOUNT OF ANNUAL SALES ON CREDIT $

The foregoing statement (both sides) has been carefully read by the undersigned (both the printed and written matter), and is, to my knowledge in all respects complete, accurate and truthful. It discloses to you the true state of my (our) financial condition on the ____ day of ____ 19____. Since that time there has been no material unfavorable change in my (our) financial condition; and if any such change takes place I (we) will give you notice. Until such notice is given you are to regard this as a continuing statement. The figures submitted are not estimated. They have been taken from my (our) books and physical inventory taken as on date shown.

Name of Firm or Corporation
Date of Signing Statement Street City State
Witness Signed by (Owner, Partner or Officer of Corporation Must Sign)
Residence Address of Witness Title

DO NOT WRITE BELOW THIS LINE

Making Credit Inquiries

60. Make the letter requesting credit information from references compact and courteous, and offer to reciprocate favors. If definite information is desired, ask specific questions or enclose a credit information form to be filled in and returned by the reference. Usually this type of letter is a form letter.

Soliciting information from trade references:

(*a*)

Dear Mr. Blank:

John Simpson, 874 Locust Street, Mobile, Alabama, wishes to open an account with us, with a credit limit of $200. He has given your name as a reference.

We shall, of course, appreciate any information you can give us regarding the ability of this person to meet his obligations promptly and any other facts that will help us in determining the amount of credit to extend.

At any time that we can serve you in a similar way, we shall gladly do so.

Very truly yours,

JOHN HARRIS CO.

(*b*)

Gentlemen:

We shall be grateful to you if you will answer the questions listed below, giving us your frank opinion of the character, habits, business ability, and financial standing of the person or firm named.

We shall appreciate a prompt reply and hope that there may be an occasion soon when we can reciprocate your kindness.

NAME OF PERSON OR FIRM......................

LOCATION..

Is he now a customer of yours?...........................
How long has he done business with you?................
What credit do you extend?.................................
Does he take cash discounts?...........................
If not, does he meet bills promptly when due?............
Give an idea of the extensions he asks for, if any..........

....

If not against your policy, state how much he owes you now, and what part, if any, is past due.....................

....

Has your experience been generally satisfactory with this customer?..
Have you any reason to suspect that he is not as good a risk just now as he has been in the past?...................
Other data bearing on credit risk.....................

....

....

Very truly yours,

THE ECLIPSE CO.

(*c*)

Gentlemen:

We have been referred to you by
of   as being in a position to give us information for our guidance in extending credit.

If it is not contrary to your policy, kindly complete and return the form below in the enclosed, self-addressed stamped envelope.

Any information furnished will, of course, be treated in strict confidence. If at any time we can serve you in like manner, we shall gladly do so.

Very truly yours,

RADIO CORPORATION OF AMERICA

Sold since: ________________ To: ________________
Terms: ____
Largest amount owing recently: ________________
Total amount now owing: ______________________
Amount past due: ____________________________
Pays: ______________________________________
Other information: ___________________________
____
____

Signature: __________________

Soliciting information from bank references:

Gentlemen:

Mr. John Doe, of 576 South Park Avenue, Kankakee, Illinois, has given your name as reference in connection with the establishment of credit.

In addition to the regular charge account, our credit privileges are to include the occasional cashing of personal checks up to $200. Any information as to his financial responsibility that you can give us will be appreciated, and, we assure you, will not be disclosed.

We thank you for your attention.

Very truly yours,
HOTEL ROOSEVELT

Answering Credit Inquiries

61a. Be sure that your letter answering a credit inquiry gives a definite and specific opinion of the customer. The opinion should be frank, concise, truthful, and based on facts. However, so word the letter that you, as the writer, assume no legal responsibility.

Favorable response:

Gentlemen:

We are glad to answer your letter of February 12, in which you inquire about our experience with John Simpson, 874 Locust Street, Mobile, Alabama.

Mr. Simpson has had a credit account with us for the past five years and has always discounted his bills promptly. With us he has a credit limit of $500.

Mr. Simpson is one of our best customers.

Yours very truly,

THE B. C. JONES CO.

b. When the reply is unfavorable, make the letter more cautious, impersonal, and guarded. Statements may often be general, and the name and the address of the customer may frequently be omitted.

Unfavorable response:

Gentlemen:

In reply to your letter of February 10, we are sorry to report that our experience with the firm mentioned has been unsatisfactory.

During the three years we have served this firm, it has failed to discount its bills and several times has caused us difficulty in collection. At the present time, it owes us a considerable amount on past-due accounts.

Yours very truly,

SMITH & CO.

Accepting Credit

62. State that credit has been granted and to what amount, explain the terms of payment, and express appreciation for the account. Tie the customer to the house by creating good will and by emphasizing service (for example, a statement of store policy, an expression of friendly coöperation, a reflection of the personality of the store, an explanation of credit facilities and the manner of using the charge accounts, a helpful reference to store departments and directories, in-

formation about deliveries, or a general expression of good will. In letters to dealers, specific dealer-service helps may be utilized; see p. 123). In some cases, this letter will begin the customer's credit education.

Dear Mrs. Smith:

Granting credit: We are very appreciative of the opportunity to establish a monthly charge account, with a credit limit of $50, for your future convenience.

Service: It permits us to serve you to better advantage by enabling us to give you personal service and individual attention.

Terms and explanation: On or about the first of each month, you will receive an itemized statement of your purchases of the previous month, which is payable in full during the early part of the month.

Enclosed you will find our regular signature card. We shall appreciate your signature and that of all other authorized purchasers for the protection of your account and for identification in cashing checks.

Good will: We hope that our dealings will develop into a permanent friendship that will prove pleasant and highly satisfactory to you.

Yours very truly,

BARKER BROS., INC.

Dear Mrs. Johnson:

We take pleasure in informing you that we have opened a charge account in your name.

A statement will be sent the first of each month, and full settlement is required by the tenth unless other arrangements are made in advance.

It is our policy to place a limit on every account. On this particular account, credit has been granted to the amount of $25.

We are enclosing your Charga-Plate, a modern device to save your time and increase your pleasure in shopping at The Avon. When making a purchase, simply hand this plate to the salesperson, and with it she will print your name and address on the sales check—always correct. For your own protection, please sign the back of your Charga-Plate now; then no one else can use it.

We sincerely hope you will enjoy using your Charga-Plate and that you will always carry it to make your shopping at The Avon faster and safer.

Very truly yours,

THE AVON

Refusing Credit

63. Letters declining requests for credit usually incorporate the following points:

a. Acknowledgment of receipt of credit information.

b. Analysis of the situation, beginning with the favorable aspects and tactfully leading to the less favorable. Plain statement of the firm's decision. (If the applicant lacks ability or willingness to pay, he should frankly but considerately be told so; this is part of the function of credit education.)

c. Offer of the firm's coöperation, and suggestion, if possible, of a practical solution of the applicant's problem. (The letter should leave the opportunity for the applicant to reopen the matter with the store's credit manager or with the manager of the credit bureau.)

d. Attempt to secure the applicant's business on a cash basis. (Always leave open the way for future business.)

REFUSING CREDIT

Declining on insufficient information:

Dear Mr. Bowman:

Your application for a charge account with our store is a compliment to our efforts to give good value and good service, and we sincerely thank you for the preference shown.

As is the usual custom before a new account is opened, we have striven to acquire information that would serve as a basis for credit. Such information as we have thus far obtained does not permit us to form a definite conclusion, and for the present, therefore, it is not possible to pass favorably on your request.

We realize that misunderstandings sometimes occur through trifling matters which, if particulars were known, would have little or no bearing on the consideration of one's credit standing, and if you feel that our action is not warranted, we shall be glad to have you call so that a better understanding may be achieved.

In the meantime, we hope that we may still be permitted to supply your wants on a cash basis and that we may continue to merit your good will.

Very truly yours,[3]

Declining on derogatory information:

Dear Mr. Simpson:

Your recent application for a charge account is gratefully acknowledged, and it has been our pleasure to give it the most careful consideration.

The information that we have been able to secure, however, is not sufficient to permit us to form a definite conclusion at the present time, as the Blank Credit Bureau, which is the central clearing house for all Blank retail credit data, discloses some question about your credit accounts.

[3] By permission of the National Retail Credit Association.

May we suggest that you call personally at the Bureau, third floor, the Chamber of Commerce Building, and see Mr. Roe, the Secretary, who will be glad to go over your records with you and adjust any errors?

We appreciate the opportunity you have given us to serve you, and we thank you for your cash patronage. You will find our personnel ready to assist you at all times, and it is our hope that this pleasant relationship will continue.

Very truly yours,[4]

Business Promotion Letters

64a. The purpose of the business promotion letter is to secure new customers and to get as much trade as possible from old ones. Through attempting to be of service to the reader, the letter sells indirectly, although it does not appear to be a sales letter. It is a friendly and personal letter that creates good will in addition to keeping the name of the firm before the customers.

Dear Mrs. Allan:

May we join your other neighbors in saying:

"WELCOME TO NASHVILLE!"

As soon as you get settled, won't you drop in and get acquainted—whether or not you're ready to buy?

You'll find that we're the kind of store you undoubtedly patronized back home. In the half century we've been in business here, we've earned a reputation for sound quality—style leadership—bed-rock values. Ask some of your neighbors about our store.

Because you will also want to enjoy the convenience of a charge account, we invite you to call at our credit office and open your account.

Cordially yours,

JOSEPH FRANK & SON[5]

[4] *Ibid.*
[5] *Ibid.*

b. The business promotion letter is used in a variety of ways:

(1) Soliciting new business.

Dear Mr. Smith:

Some time ago, we forwarded to you a booklet describing in some detail the Universal Air Travel Plan. Since that time an event has occurred that materially changes the significance of the Air Travel Plan to American business.

United Air Lines' fares have been reduced again, bringing the over-all reduction since 1941 to 24 per cent. Air travel now costs substantially less than first-class rail plus Pullman transportation.

In view of the situation, you undoubtedly will wish to review again the advantages of the Air Travel Plan as applied to your own business. In the first seven months of this year, almost 7,000 business firms have adopted the plan. Today, well over 25,000 Air Travel Plans are in active use by American industry.

If your copy of the booklet, which describes the Air Travel Plan in detail, has been lost or mislaid, a replacement will be supplied promptly upon request. Or if you desire further information concerning the application of the plan to your own business, we shall be pleased to have a competent representative call at your convenience.

Very truly yours,

UNITED AIR LINES

(2) Soliciting new charge accounts.

Dear Mr. Elder:

To you as one of our "new" families we extend our congratulations and a cordial invitation to open a charge account for your convenience in making the many purchases necessary in equipping your new home.

With a charge account your shopping is simplified and your time saved. The intimate contact gained is of mutual advantage. It gives you prestige—for a good credit standing in the community is to be greatly valued.

Your account is ready for you to use as soon as you wish. Just say "charge it" and receive our most prompt attention.

Yours very truly,

M. L. PARKER COMPANY[6]

(3) **Building good will by offering service, such as sales or service aids, educational assistance, public service, or general expressions of friendly interest.**

Gentlemen:

If you've ever had any complaints about slow deliveries from your customers, we believe you'll want a supply of the attached Air Express Rush labels. We'll be glad to send as many as you can use, as explained below.

We've talked to many people whose buying problems are similar to those of your customers. And we've discovered that often when they need Fastest Way service—which calls for shipment by Air Express—they don't get it. Why? Because of the tendency to scrawl "Rush" or "Hurry" on orders without explaining exactly how to ship. You've probably received many such orders in your own organization.

So we had these labels made up. Notice that they come in perforated sheets—twelve on each, which makes them ideal for insertion in catalogs, price lists, or other printed material distributed to your customers. You can have them tipped in, using the instruction part at the top for pasting or just inserted loose in a convenient section. Perhaps your catalog has a standard page

[6] By permission of the National Retail Credit Association.

on Air Express or a section devoted to shipping information. Either of these would be an ideal place for the label sheet. Or you may wish to mail the sheets directly to your customers, or have your representatives leave them as they make their rounds. Customers can then decide whether to put them in your catalog or keep them in a handy place.

In any case, these labels can help a lot in overcoming needlessly slow shipments. For when an order comes in bearing one of these little rush warnings, you always know exactly how your customer wants his shipment sent. And fast deliveries have a way of building good will, as well as gaining extra time for production.

Of course, you'll also find the labels handy when sending out rush orders to your own suppliers. Just keep them where orders are made out in your organization, and they'll help you get your materials in on time.

To secure whatever quantity you wish of these label sheets, simply fill out the enclosed postage-paid reply card and have it mailed to us. There's no cost or obligation involved. We'll send them out as soon as we receive your request.

Very truly yours,

RAILWAY EXPRESS AGENCY

(4) Keeping accounts active. Letters may be sent on the occasions of special sales, seasons, the beginnings of the buying seasons, birthdays, graduations, anniversaries, school openings, and the like. (Cf. the continuous follow-up sales series, p. 255.)

Dear Mrs. Nikoden:

Wouldn't you like to select unhurriedly this year Christmas gifts for the men on your list?

In our shop at 900 North Michigan the very atmosphere bids you shop leisurely, and you may park your car in this neighborhood without fear of being disturbed. There are no parking rules to worry you.

Many handsome gifts for men are on display, and our salesmen are eager to be helpful. Their knowledge gained from experience in serving men the year round is at your disposal.

I really believe you will enjoy gift shopping in this conveniently located little store, and you may be sure you will be welcomed most cordially.

Very sincerely,

CAPPER & CAPPER[7]

Dear Mrs. Summers:

Don't breathe a word of this . . . but we're trying to bribe you.

See the enclosed check? It's yours—to spend at A. Hirsh and Son during the month of November. There is only one condition. . . .

We want you to shop early—before December 1!

If we could change places for a while you'd realize why we make this offer. Business goes on as usual during November, and then, BANG, we're swamped.

It's hard on us and not fair to you because you don't get either the service or the selection.

So it's a check for you as a bribe to do your Christmas shopping early, and as an added inducement the enclosed credit card allows you to buy now and not pay one cent until NEXT YEAR.

Just put the enclosed check in your purse and write the name "A. Hirsh & Son" in your appointment book. We're expecting you—soon!

Very truly yours,

A. HIRSH & SON

[7] From *Postage and the Mailbag.*

(5) Reviving inactive accounts (discovering why a customer has ceased purchasing)[8]

Dear Mr. Freeman:

Someone has said, "To lose one's wealth is much, to lose one's health is more, but to lose one's friends is a loss that nothing can restore."

You are one of our friends that we have taken pride in serving for many years, so it is with great concern that, in looking through our credit accounts recently, we noted that you have not visited our store for many months.

We always try to be fair, and we always try to render every service within our power. But we make mistakes, and that is where we need your help. If you have received some article which is not entirely satisfactory, we shall be glad to make whatever adjustment is fair and satisfactory. Please jot us a note on the reverse side of this letter and mail it in the enclosed, stamped envelope.

We want you as a friend to tell us how we may better serve you.

Very truly yours,

BALLOU AND FRIML

(6) Expressing appreciation of the first order or purchase or of any business, which may result in future sales.

Dear Mrs. Delaney:

We're happy to have had the opportunity of serving you recently on "The Challenger."

Your patronage is genuinely appreciated, and we extend to you our sincere "thank you."

We hope your trip was thoroughly enjoyable and that you will soon travel again over the Union Pacific Railroad.

[8] See "Inviting Claims," p. 204.

When you do, our San Jose office will gladly assist you with your travel plans, tickets, or reservations. The address is 206 First National Bank Building, Santa Clara and First Streets . . . phone Ballard 1634.

Cordially yours,

UNION PACIFIC RAILROAD

(7) Expressing appreciation of present good-paying accounts or of good paid-out accounts; account solicitation letters for paid-up budget accounts.

Dear Mr. Brown:

This is a credit letter . . . but it's one you'll enjoy reading!

One way we have of finding out whether we should give more liberal credit to certain of our customers is to notice the way they meet their regular payments.

You have made a fine record of prompt payment in handling your account, and we would like to show our appreciation by extending you the extra credit privileges we reserve for our most preferred customers.

You may have noticed in recent weeks the fine new lines of merchandise with which our store is now stocked. We would like to suggest that the next time you drop in you take a closer look at the sporting goods, sportswear, auto supplies, garden and home necessities on display—any merchandise that you wish to have may be bought right on your present account.

We urge you to take advantage of this special invitation now, because we are very anxious for our regular customers to have the first selection of our many bargains.

Very truly yours,

B. F. GOODRICH SILVERTOWN STORES

Dear Mr. Porter:

Thank you for your check of $25 received March 19 to pay your account in full.

Your friendship and loyalty have contributed much to the progress of our store, and it is our aim to keep your good will.

No doubt, other needs in your home will arise as time goes on, and it is our hope that you will think then of ANDERSON'S, the store which is "JUST BIG ENOUGH TO SERVE YOU RIGHT."

Best wishes to you.

Cordially yours,

ANDERSON FURNITURE COMPANY[9]

[9] By permission of the National Retail Credit Association.

[65]

Collection Letters

The Classes of Customers

65a. Class A: The good risk. The good risk is highly rated with respect to his financial ability. His paying habits, however, may be prompt or slow. Because his credit limit is high, he is given the mildest and most lenient treatment of the three classes; the operation of the collection system takes a longer period of time than for the other two classes; and more notifications and letters are sent.

Class B: The medium or fair risk. The medium risk if a customer whose financial ability and paying habits justify a credit limit somewhere between that of the good risk and the poor risk. His ability to pay is greater than that of the poor risk, and his paying habits are better. The creditor is more lenient with him than with the poor risk, allowing a longer interval of time for the operation of the system and sending more notifications and letters.

Class C: The poor risk. The poor risk is a customer whose ability to pay and whose paying habits justify only a small credit limit. He is permitted but a short time for payment; and when he fails to pay, the collection system operates quickly.

b. Some firms classify debtors into the following more analytically descriptive groups: prompt, chronically slow, good but in temporary financial difficulties, callous, dishonest, and insolvent. This classification makes necessary closer adaptation of the collection

procedure to the delinquent debtor than the simpler A,B,C classification.

The Stages in the Collection Procedure

66. There are four stages in the collection procedure through which accounts pass, although not every account necessarily passes through all four stages. Resale of goods, service, or credit responsibility may be employed in any stage.

Reminder. The stage of reminder assumes that failure to pay is due to forgetfulness or negligence. The delinquent account is brought to the debtor's attention by means of formal reminders and brief letters of reminder.

You have perhaps allowed this account to escape your notice. Please give it your attention.

Just another friendly reminder of our terms, which are—ordinarily—monthly in full.

This statement is sent to you for comparison and as a reminder of mutual understanding as to terms.

Dear Mr. Joyne:

Your account with us shows a balance of $... which is somewhat past due. This is undoubtedly an oversight, and we therefore call it to your attention.

You may overlook this matter again if you put our letter aside; so why not pin a check to it right now and send it to us?

Very truly yours,

W. A. SHEAFFER PEN CO.

Dear Mr. Taylor:

An alarm clock and a collection letter are very similar—neither ever intends to offend; they merely remind us of something we were going to do anyway.

[66]

So will you accept this friendly reminder of your intention to send us a check for your February account of $20?

Very truly yours,

THE B. R. BAKER CO.[1]

Discussion. The stage of discussion assumes that the debtor's failure to pay is due to the fact that he is in trouble, that he has a good reason for not paying, or that unusual circumstances are responsible for the delay. The letters of this stage offer assistance and try to get either payment or a reply explaining the debtor's reason, stating his difficulty, or telling when he expects to pay.

Gentlemen:

You are one of our new customers, and this is our first credit relation with you. Our three statements and our letters of (date) and (date) have as yet been unanswered. This would indicate that something is wrong.

Did we not come to a satisfactory credit understanding?

Have we made some mistake in the charge?

How do you wish us to handle your account?

By all means, be frank in telling us if any mistake has occurred, for you will find us more than willing to correct it.

Very truly yours,

THE B. F. GOODRICH RUBBER CO.

Dear Mrs. Morely:

In the past few months you have made only partial payments on your account, and at this rate, your account will not be balanced for some time.

[1] By permission of the National Retail Credit Association.

We realize, however, that there may be a very good reason why you cannot pay in full. We should appreciate, therefore, an interview with you so that some definite arrangement can be made.

Very truly yours,

THE BON MARCHÉ

Gentlemen:

A few days ago we reminded you that payment on your account with us had been overlooked.

The statement which we are enclosing shows that as yet your check covering the past-due amount has not been received.

If there is any reason for withholding payment, will you not let us know so that an immediate adjustment can be made?

If there is no reason for delay, we should appreciate your remittance at this time.

Very truly yours,

REMINGTON RAND BUSINESS
SERVICE INC.

Appeal. The stage of appeal assumes that the delinquent debtor needs urgent prodding. The letters of this stage attempt to induce payment by appealing to motives such as sympathy, pride, justice and fairness, honor, and self-interest.

Gentlemen:

When your account was opened with us, we had every reason to believe you would pay it promptly when it became due.

In making the usual credit investigations, we discovered that all of those with whom you had done business spoke very highly of you in a personal way, and declared that you would meet your obligations as they fell due.

It is, therefore, difficult for us to understand why you have not taken care of our account amounting to $. . . .

Before investigating further your manner of making payment to others, in which investigation we should, of course, have to state what our experience has been with you, we want to give you another opportunity to pay your long past-due account with us.

It would not favorably impress those who have recommended you so highly to learn that our experience has not fully justified the unqualified recommendations which they gave to us.

We shall expect your check by the seventh.

Very truly yours,

THE B. F. GOODRICH RUBBER CO.

Demand. The stage of demand assumes that the delinquent debtor does not intend to pay, is extremely negligent, or is irresponsible. Consequently, payment is demanded, and the disagreeable consequences of nonpayment—the bringing of a suit or the turning-over of the account to a collection agency—are threatened. Drafts are sometimes used at this stage. However, good will may be retained by an attitude of fairness, by restraint in phrasing, and by showing the debtor that the firm has been patient and considerate.

Gentlemen:

The complete file of correspondence in connection with your account, as shown on the attached statement, has been referred to me with a request that permission be given to turn over your account to our attorney.

When I approved your order, I did so because I felt that you would meet your obligations promptly; and although I am naturally disappointed to learn that your account is not paid, still I think I was right in my judgment. I am sure there must be some unusual circumstance surrounding this account, as I cannot conceive of anyone's wilfully neglecting to answer letter after letter, especially in view of our liberal attitude.

Further action will mean considerable expense and embarrassment for you. I want, therefore, to make this personal appeal to you to send us a check for your account, or make some arrangement whereby payment will be completed within a reasonable length of time.

I am enclosing a stamped, self-addressed envelope, and shall appreciate it if you will send your remittance to us at once.

Very truly yours,

REMINGTON RAND BUSINESS SERVICE INC.

Novelty letters may be employed in any stage.

Dear Mr. Doe:

Please send us a check in payment of your past-due account—either a *real check* or a *pencil check* in one of the spaces below:

( ) Here's all of it—SHUT UP!

( ) Here's part of it to show my heart's in the right place.

( ) Can't possibly make a payment today—will positively send one by ______________________.

( ) Enclosed is $__________; will send this amount each __________ around the __________ until paid.

( ) Don't intend to pay unless I'm sued for it.

We await your reply by return mail.

Sincerely,

THE CREDIT BUREAU[2]

[2] By permission of the National Retail Credit Association.

[66]

TIME *The Weekly Newsmagazine* • CHICAGO • NEW YORK
CIRCULATION DEPARTMENT: 330 EAST 22ND STREET, CHICAGO, ILLINOIS

Dear Subscriber:

There is only one point in sending you this pin – – – – – –

See a pin and pick it up, and all the day you'll have good luck.

– – – – – – to help you pin your check to the enclosed statement for your TIME subscription and mail it to me promptly in the enclosed envelope.

And here is a stamp in anticipation of your willingness to mail your check today.

With thanks for your promptness and for your interest in TIME.

Cordially,

Charles Mason

Credit Manager

CM-G

* The above letter is reproduced by permission of *Time*.

Mrs. J. J. Jones
No. 1 Pedro Place
Phoenix, Arizona

Dear Mrs. Jones:

In the Navajo Indian language this is the "horse". It stands for a "journey". We hope you will soon journey in to see us about your account.

This is the bear track. It means "good omen". Your visit will be a good omen, and we feel certain a mutually satisfactory plan will be easy to arrange. If you can't come in, won't you telephone now?

Sincerely

Dear Mr. Johns:

Do you remember the days when you tied a bit of string on your finger—just to remind you of something you didn't want to forget?

Perhaps you have given up the string habit, and sometimes some little thing is forgotten.

As in the days of yore, tie the bit of string on your finger now as a reminder—NOT TO FORGET—to pay the milk bill.

We hope you enjoy the smile in our letter and that we may have the pleasure of hearing from you promptly.

Very truly yours,

CARLSON-FRINK CO.[3]

[3] By permission of the National Retail Credit Association.

Dear Mr. Dallas:

Before getting into the busy holiday season, we know that you will want to give us a report on the enclosed bill which has gone unpaid because of an oversight or other reasons. For your convenience, we are enclosing an addressed, stamped envelope for the return of this sheet after you have checked off the following:

( ) I mailed you a check yesterday.

( ) I will mail you a check ______________.

( ) I am writing the reason for nonpayment on the reverse side.

Thanking you for the prompt attention which we are confident you will give this matter, we wish you a very pleasant holiday season.

Sincerely yours,

ARTHUR A. EVERTS CO.[4]

Formal Reminders

67a. Use a formal reminder to remind the debtor in a mild and inoffensive way that his account is overdue.[5]

b. Formal reminders are brief and impersonal in tone and expressed in stereotyped language. They appear to be a matter of routine, contain no personal appeal, and make no personal reference. They courteously refer to the overdue account and call attention to the fact that the bill is unpaid.

c. Formal reminders are of various types:

(1) A bill or statement on which is written, printed, or stamped such expressions as:

[4] *Ibid.*

[5] Note that in the stage of reminder, letters, as well as formal reminders, may also be used; see pp. 159-60.

FORMAL REMINDERS

Account past due.
Please remit.
Please.
Reminder.
The above account is past due.
A prompt remittance will be appreciated.
Please give this your attention.
May we have a check, please?
Second notice.
Duplicate.

(2) **A brief reminder without salutation or signature, printed on a card or slip and clipped or pasted to the statement.**

You have perhaps allowed this account to escape your notice. Please give it your attention.

No doubt, it is an oversight that this account, which is now past due, has not been paid. Will you please give it your prompt attention?

We respectfully request your immediate attention to this past-due account.

E. C. Hodges & Company respectfully call attention to the enclosed statement, which, no doubt, has been overlooked.

This statement is sent to you for comparison and a reminder of mutual understanding as to terms.

Just another friendly reminder of our terms which are—ordinarily—monthly in full.

Possibly you have overlooked the past-due portion of the enclosed statement. Should any adjustments be necessary, we shall cheerfully give them our attention.

(3) **A printed form with no inside address, salutation, or complimentary close, containing blank spaces for the insertion of the name and address of the customer, the amount owed, and the date of purchase. It is generally printed on a card, and**

the spaces may be filled in with ink or by typewriter.

Your account of .... amounting to $..... is now past due. Please give this your attention.

HOLLINGTON COMPANY

We wish to call attention to your account of ...., amounting to $...... Your prompt attention will be appreciated.

LARSON BROTHERS

(4) A typewritten or multigraphed form with blank spaces in which all necessary information may be inserted. This form contains a salutation and a complimentary close, and is personally signed.

Dear Sir:

Your attention is respectfully directed to your account of $ covering invoices shown on our recent statement.

A prompt remittance will be appreciated.

Yours very truly,

Dear Sir:

Your account is now months past due. Kindly remit your check for this amount.

Amount past due $

Very truly yours,

Dear Sir:

We are sending you a copy of your invoice of in order that you may check it as to its correctness. On our books the amount appears as unpaid.

Should there be any error, please notify us, and we shall gladly correct it.

Very truly yours,

(5) Other printed forms.

PLEASE $10.56

KEITH-O'BRIEN, INC.
56 EAST THIRD SOUTH
SALT LAKE CITY UTAH

Mr. R. A. Wise
2525 January
Salt Lake City, Utah

4M—9-33

STANDARD FURNITURE COMPANY
"The House of Quality"
7 to 15 South Main Street
SALT LAKE CITY, UTAH

A gentle reminder that you promised to make a payment at this time. It will be most welcome.

STANDARD FURNITURE CO.
Collection Department—X

PLEASE accept this as a friendly reminder that your account is past due
An early remittance will be appreciated.

Raleigh Haberdasher
WASHINGTON, D C

DEPARTMENT OF ACCOUNTS.
THIRD FLOOR

[67]

HERE IS A RECORD OF YOUR ACCOUNT: DATE January 25, 19 __

Your prompt payment is solicited in the same friendly manner as is your patronage. -- Both are essential to our success.

Arthur McFarlane, Pres.-Mgr.
Ray R. McFarlane, Sec.-Treas.

NOW DUE	30 DAYS PAST DUE	60 DAYS PAST DUE	90 DAYS PAST DUE	__ DAYS PAST DUE	TOTAL AMOUNT DUE
$16.23	$9.67	$3.32	$1.56		$30.78

McFARLANE
Fuel & Stoker Co.
271 South State St.
Dial 4-5638
Dial 4-5639
Credit Terms—
Net 30 Days

Mr. Henry J. Dunn
4362 Legal Avenue
St. Charles, Mo.

Treat
Your Credis
as a
Sacred Trust

CREDIT -- "MAN'S CONFIDENCE IN MAN"

A second friendly reminder

Our recent reminder of your past due account has not met with a response.

The amount shown here is for the two previous months' purchases. May we please have your check?

SOCONY-VACUUM OIL COMPANY
INCORPORATED

THE AMOUNT IS
$57.67

Mr. George M. Watson,
5476 Hendricks Drive,
Apt. 9,
Watsonville, Tenn.

FORM [illegible]
(1-41)-

d. If the first reminder secures no response, another, still impersonal but somewhat more insistent and stronger in tone, may be sent.

Dear Sir:

We again wish to call to your attention your past-due account for the month of ...., statement of which was sent to you several weeks ago.

We shall appreciate your check in payment of this account.

Amount past due $..........

Very truly yours,

Dear Sir:

Your invoice of .... for $.........., now past due for two months, is still unpaid. On .... we wrote you about this, but have received no reply. We desire again to call your attention to the need for settlement.

If any adjustments should be necessary, we hope that you will notify us immediately.

Very truly yours,

e. Never send the following kind of formal reminder, unless the customer's business is no longer desired.

THIRD DELINQUENT NOTICE!

Evidently you do not believe in the "Golden Rule." Your attitude indicates a desire to evade payment of a just obligation. Was it a mistake to invest in your integrity? PLEASE REMIT.

The Structure of the Collection Letter

68. The collection letter contains the following elements:

Opening: The opening must grasp the reader's attention. An individual and personal contact is more likely to interest the reader than one that is hackneyed, routine, or uninteresting.

Details of account: The letter states the amount due, the length of time the bill has run, and what it is for.

Appeal: The letter appeals to certain motives that give the debtor reasons why he should pay and that make him feel he ought to pay.

Close: The clincher must stimulate the debtor to definite and immediate action—to pay the bill or to give an explanation. Participial, apologetic, vague, or indefinite closes are weak and ineffective.

Dear Mr. Doe:

Opening: When your account was opened with us, we had every reason to believe you would pay it promptly when it became due.

In making the usual credit investigations, we discovered that all of those with whom you had done business spoke very highly of you in a personal way, and declared that you would meet your obligations as they fell due.

Details of account: It is, therefore, difficult for us to understand why you have not taken care of our account amounting to $80, which is now two months past due.

Appeal: Before investigating further your manner of making payment to others, in which investigation we should, of course, have to state what our experience has been with you, we want to give you another opportunity to pay your long past-due account with us.

It would not favorably impress those who have recommended you so highly to learn that our experience has not fully justified the unqualified recommendations which they gave to us.

Close: We shall expect your check by the tenth.

Very truly yours,

THE B. F. GOODRICH RUBBER CO.

The Collection Appeals

69. By appealing to motives, collection letters in the stages of appeal and demand give the debtor reasons why he should pay and make him feel that he ought to pay. Resale of goods, service, or credit responsibility may be combined with the appeal.

Sympathy. The appeal to sympathy tries to induce payment by making the debtor feel that because of his failure to pay his bill the creditor is suffering financially or is laboring under needless burdens. The weakest of the appeals, it is used only in the first personal letter. Whenever it results in a loss of dignity, it should not be employed. More effective than reference to financial loss is a persuasive appeal for the debtor's coöperation in helping the firm conduct its business efficiently and free from mere bookkeeping burdens.

Gentlemen:

In going over our ledgers, we find a large number of very small balances, which have been standing for some time. On your account there is a little balance of $....., which seems to have been entirely overlooked.

We are making an effort to eliminate these matters from our records and would very much appreciate your helping us by sending a check for the small amount due on your account.

Very truly yours,
THE APEX CO.

Pride. The appeal to pride arouses the debtor's pride in his own good business name and in his reputation among his business associates. It is effective with business men who conduct their affairs in a businesslike manner, with well-rated firms, and with individuals of high rating. This appeal is used less frequently with habitually slow or callous debtors.

Dear Mr. Lants:

You are justly proud of your business standing, and proud of the reputation you have among your business associates as a man who meets his obligations squarely and discharges them promptly. Every dealing we have had with you in the past indicates that.

For these reasons, we feel sure you will realize it is to your best interests, as well as to ours, that you settle at once that April account amounting to $...... and thereby avoid compelling us to take drastic action.

Your business reputation is entirely too good to be exposed to injury by continued neglect and carelessness.

Enclose a check in this letter, put it in the attached envelope, and start it on its way to us—now.

Very truly yours,

THE B. F. GOODRICH RUBBER CO.

Justice and fairness. The purpose of this appeal is to make the debtor feel that he is not treating the firm fairly. The creditor has delivered satisfactory goods or service, and the debtor should in justice make prompt payment. If it is shown that the house is impartial in all its dealings and makes no exceptions for a favored few, the appeal is effective with customers who take unearned discounts.

Gentlemen:

You have plenty of bills of your own to collect, and you know how good you feel when a man pays up promptly—how you would like to do him favors.

That's the way we have always felt toward you, and we want you to let us feel the same way this year. We want you to pay your overdue account now, before it gets any older.

Won't you go to your bookkeeper and say:

"Send a check to the B. F. Goodrich Rubber Company today"?

Thank you.

Yours very truly,

THE B. F. GOODRICH RUBBER CO.

Dear Subscriber:

Because this letter is about money anyway, I thought I might start off by reminding you that . . .

TIME is spending well over 25¢ a word in its editorial department alone this year—to make sure we bring you the full meaning of each significant event, and to make sure every word you read in *TIME* is straight and true and reliable.

TIME spends more than twice as much per word as any other news journal in the world—and the only reason we can offer you such a service for less than its million dollar cost is that so many other subscribers share the expense.

Your share of the expense of *TIME*'s service for eight months is $2.67—and it would be a great help if you could let us have your check today.

Very truly yours,

TIME

Statistical P.S. Your $2.67 will just about pay for the editorial research, the writing and rewriting, the checking, the re-checking and editing of *eleven words in one issue of TIME.*

Dear Mr. Watson:

Monthly charge accounts for automotive products are a service that McKale's is happy to extend to certain preferred customers at no additional cost.

We are glad to see that you have been making regular use of your account and hope you are enjoying the many conveniences it affords. We are anxious that you continue to receive and enjoy this service.

In order to make this possible, however, it is necessary that our customers coöperate with us by paying their accounts in full promptly every month. Your account is past due $75 for charges made in June.

The immediate payment of this balance will insure the continued convenience of your account and will be sincerely appreciated.

Very truly yours,

McKALE'S, INC.[6]

Honor. The appeal to honor stresses the contractual obligation. It shows that the house regards the credit contract seriously and has fulfilled its part of the contract, and that it is now up to the customer to do the same.

Gentlemen:

It is rather discouraging to observe that the amount, $......, under your name, represents the first transaction we have enjoyed with your establishment. The sale was made under terms of "two per cent ten days, net thirty."

Perhaps you have not stopped to consider that when one man engages another to perform a service or deliver a commodity, he enters into a contract. If business is to be sound, that contract must be held sacred by both parties as far as personal responsibility can go.

In view of our having written you previously, we are most confident that this letter will not remain unanswered, even if for some reason unknown to us you find it impossible to pay.

Yours very truly,

THE B. F. GOODRICH RUBBER CO.

[6] By permission of the National Retail Credit Association.

THE COLLECTION APPEALS

Dear Mr. Doe:

"His word is as good as his bond."

That's the principle upon which honest men based their credit dealings in the "good old days."

No note.

No written contract.

Just a man's word—that's all.

And men turned heaven and earth to keep it.

You and your family were furnished our merchandise in October on the strength of your word to pay when due.

No security.

No collateral.

Just your word—and our faith in you.

What would you do if circumstances were reversed and we had been in your debt since October?

We did our part. Have you done yours?

Put yourself in our place—then let us hear from you.

Very truly yours,

A. HARRIS & COMPANY[7]

Self-interest. The customer is shown that it is to his own personal advantage to pay now, that prompt payment improves his credit standing and enables the firm to sell at lower prices. His attention is called to the periodical reporting of delinquents to credit associations. By informing or reminding him of the interchange of credit information between sellers, the letter indicates how his failure to make prompt payment affects his credit standing with other firms as well as with the writer's. However, care must be

[7] By permission of the National Retail Credit Association.

taken to avoid any suggestion of blacklisting, which will render the creditor liable to legal punishment.

Dear Mr. Weston:

You, like millions of others, are probably looking forward to using your credit when you do your Christmas buying.

The first step in maintaining a good credit record is to pay each account when it is due. The files of the Credit Bureau contain the credit record of everyone who has used his credit. Every merchant who is a member of the Credit Bureau has access to these records.

Since credit is extended on the promptness with which one pays his accounts, we wish to call to your attention the amount we are now carrying past due on our books for you.

The amount is $109.69. Payment of this amount will enable us to report your account to the Credit Bureau as having been paid to date. Your immediate attention to this will pay you dividends when applying for credit with other merchants.

Very truly yours,

CUSSINS & FEARN CO.[8]

Fear. The appeal to fear indicates the disagreeable things that will happen if the debtor does not pay his account by a certain date. It makes a threat to sue, to place the account in the hands of an attorney or a collection agency, or to send a personal collector. Although it is the strongest of the appeals, the customer's trade may still be retained by restraint in the phrasing of the appeal.

Dear Mr. Jones:

Your Air Travel Credit Account continues to show a past-due balance of $387.92, although several requests have previously been made for payment.

[8] By permission of the National Retail Credit Association.

It is appreciated that present-day conditions of employment do force some of our customers to set aside their invoices which, during normal times, would be handled and paid promptly. This possibly is the reason for your account being delinquent.

Since it has always been our policy to accept only the highest type of individuals and companies on our Air Travel Plan of Credit, we do not feel too negligent in having allowed your account to become ninety days past due. Considering your excellent credit standing at the time you subscribed to the Plan, cancelation of your account as required by our policy does not seem in order.

Your check of $387.92 forwarded in the attached self-addressed, stamped envelope will allow us to continue the privileges afforded you under the Credit Plan. Having the remittance in our office within the next five days will re-establish the account on a current basis.

Very truly yours,

UNITED AIR LINES

Gentlemen:

During the past several months, we have had considerable correspondence with you regarding your delinquent account, in an earnest endeavor to induce you to remit the balance.

When matters of this kind can be worked out on a basis of mutual coöperation, you are saved expense and embarrassment, and we can, between us, save our friendly business relationship.

It has become apparent, however, that we have been unsuccessful in this endeavor, and we must reluctantly inform you that if payment in full of this account does not arrive within ten days, we shall be obliged to refer your account to our legal department.

We sincerely hope that you will make this action unnecessary by remitting immediately.

Yours very truly,

MOORE BUSINESS FORMS, INC.

COLLECTION LETTERS

Individual and Form Letters

70a. **The collection series, composed of form letters, is mechanical, though not inflexible, in construction and operation.** It works automatically in sending notifications and letters at pre-determined intervals to the different classes of customers. It is also automatic and mechanical in regard to the particular type of notice or letter to be sent on the definite date decided upon when the system is devised. Form letters and form paragraphs are used as long as the collection cases are similar. However, the series should be changed at intervals, or a number of series should be used, so that the debtor does not receive the identical message twice.

b. **When irregularities occur, or when the need arises for adaptation to special classes or to special cases, individual letters are dictated.**

c. **The collection series is better adapted for use by department stores collecting from a large number of customers, and by wholesalers or jobbers having many small past-due accounts.** Manufacturers, wholesalers, and small retailers with a less numerous clientele find individual treatment more effective.

The Collection Series

71a. **In composing the collection series, use statements, reminders, and letters arranged in sequence, so that the tone of each successive notice or letter grows more insistent until either the debtor pays or some drastic action is threatened.**

b. **The elements of the collection follow-up system are:**

1. The number of notices or letters.
2. The time intervening between successive notices or letters, and the time needed for the operation of the complete system.

3. The consideration given to the various classes of customers.
4. The tone of the letters.

c. The collection series is adapted to the particular class of customers. Fewer notices and letters are sent to the poor risk than to the medium or good risk. The operation of the system takes a shorter period of time, and the tone and the degree of insistence progress more rapidly from the impersonal reminder to the threat.

d. An example of a collection follow-up series is given below:

Poor risk:

January 15—Purchase made.
February 1—Statement sent.
February 15—Formal reminder.
March 1—First letter.
March 15—Second letter.
April 1—Third letter.
April 15—Threat letter or personal collector.

Good risk:

January 15—Purchase made.
February 1—Bill.
February 15—Statement.
March 1—First formal reminder.
March 15—Second formal reminder.
April 1—First letter.
April 15—Second letter.
May 1—Third letter.
May 15—Fourth letter.
June 1—Threat letter.

Part Payments

72. Before sending the letter threatening suit, it is often effective to try to secure part payment and to arrange

for other payments at specified intervals.[9] Such an offer of service usually brings at least a reply from the debtor.

Dear Mr. Day:

It has been a long time since you have paid anything on your account, but we must now ask that you make settlement.

We would much prefer that this be handled in a friendly way, and for that reason we are writing to you now.

As proof of your good intentions and a desire to coöperate with us, send a remittance for as much as you can and tell us just how and when you can pay the balance.

If you will give this matter the prompt attention it deserves, we are sure a mutually satisfactory settlement can be arrived at without the necessity of costs or unpleasantness.

Yours very truly,

5 5 5, INCORPORATED[10]

Extensions of Time

73a. If the debtor advances a good reason, or if it is impossible to collect the account now,[11] grant him an extension of time. Although you grant the extension cheerfully, show the customer that such procedure is an exception to the general rule because of the good reason advanced.

Dear Mrs. Campbell:

Thank you for your letter of April 9 explaining why you have not paid your account for March. Whenever our customers are in difficulties, we appreciate their writing to us frankly.

[9] See your state code for the statute of limitations in reference to debts.

[10] By permission of the National Retail Credit Association.

[11] Because of business or financial conditions at the moment, for example, or because the debtor's income is received at widely separated intervals, or because the amount owed is too small to justify the expense of suit.

Since yours is an accommodation account, payable in full by the tenth of each month, we usually insist on strict adherence to the terms of credit. However, in view of your explanation, we are glad to grant your request for an extension of time on your account.

We shall, then, expect your check in full payment of your account on April 20.

Very truly yours,

BLANK STORES, INC.

b. If the customer advances no good reason for the extension, refuse the extension courteously but firmly. Give the reason for refusing the request.

Gentlemen:

From day to day the car shortage has become increasingly serious until, like every other manufacturer, we are obliged to load to capacity every car leaving our plant.

Although this is not a restriction laid down by the railroads, there is nothing for the shipper to do other than to coöperate in every way possible to increase shipping space. To the manufacturer who is receiving shipments in less than carload lots, double loading has, in some instances, caused delays. Our traffic department traces these shipments and does everything possible to eliminate all avoidable delays. We try to keep our customers' materials moving.

It may appear to you that a large firm should readily grant requests for extended payment whenever a shipment is delayed, and we wish it were possible for us to accommodate our friends and customers in such a matter as this; but when you stop to think of the cumulative burden of such an undertaking, you can easily see how impossible it would be for us to carry the entire load.

All our material is sold f.o.b. Middletown, and while we greatly regret delays in transit, for us to make an exception in terms in your case would obligate us to grant the same privilege to others. This we have not seen our way clear to do. We have been obliged to refuse several similar requests.

Will you, therefore, kindly pass our invoice for payment as agreed?

Very truly yours,[12]

Installments

74a. Installment letters use the same appeals and tone as other collection letters. Although installment letters are usually form letters, special cases need individual treatment. The letters appeal to fear (legal suit for non-payment) only when the debtor is a weak risk or when the product cannot be resold. There is little probability of repossessing non-durable goods, which are usually sold on short-term contracts, such as ninety days. The following specimen is a letter in the stage of reminder.

Dear Mr. Smith:

Our records indicate that we have not received a remittance in payment of the installment due on your account.

It is very important that all remittances be received at our office on the dates specified in the contract that you signed.

If you have not already remitted, please detach this notice and send it together with your regular installment payment coupon and remittance in the attached envelope.

Very truly yours,

UNDERWOOD CORPORATION

b. Letters collecting for articles sold on the installment plan are especially concerned with resale of goods, service, or credit responsibility and with retention of good will. Resale is a psychological problem. Its object is to readjust the customer's attitude of mind

[12] From *Making Letters Talk Business*, The American Rolling Mill Co.

so that for the present unfavorable situation is substituted the original feeling of satisfaction and credit responsibility, which motivated him when he first bought the goods and signed the credit contract. Repossession of goods is a forceful collection appeal. But, because repossession is an unpleasant procedure which is detrimental to good will, in order to minimize the necessity of repossessing durable goods, the creditor must keep the customer sold until payment is completed. Repossession is a doubtful procedure if the unpaid balance of the installment contract is greater than the repossession value (marketable value) of the goods.

c. The installment collection series should be so arranged that the customer does not receive the same messages twice. A series of four installment letters follows.

Letter No. 1

Dear Mr. Blank:

No doubt you have merely overlooked the monthly payment on your radio, which was due three weeks ago, and will be glad to have it called to your attention.

Some of our customers, when in arrears, make two payments at one time; and since your February installment is almost due, we suggest that you write your check for the amount of $20.50.

Very truly yours,

Letter No. 2

Dear Mr. Blank:

Your installment of $10.25 for the month of January is now four weeks past due. Surely, when you purchased your radio you intended to live up to the terms of your contract by making your payments promptly. If we have in any way failed to fulfill our part, do not hesitate to write us frankly.

Without a doubt you are getting full enjoyment from your radio, which brings right into your home the world's greatest artists, performing with all their skill and individuality as if they were actually seated before you. Think of the pleasure you derive every day from the best dance music in the land, the finest symphony music, the greatest operas, the latest news broadcasts, and the most interesting commentators.

Of course, you will send us promptly your check for the overdue payments. This is really a small amount compared with the enjoyment you are getting from your investment, isn't it?

Very truly yours,

Letter No. 3

Dear Mr. Blank:

Your neglect of your account is unfair to yourself, since it affects one of your greatest assets, your credit standing. A good credit reputation, which you certainly wish to enjoy, can be obtained only by prompt attention to your obligations. Such a reputation, even when established, will continue only while you pay your bills promptly.

Surely, you will not let failure to pay these installments deprive you of all the genuine pleasure of the nightly broadcasts. We know how much you also enjoy and appreciate the fine programs during the day, the news flashes, the helpful household hints, the interesting speeches on educational, religious, political, and financial subjects.

Really, you owe it to yourself to pay what you agreed. Send us your check for $20.50 and be spared the embarrassment that overdue installments always bring.

Very truly yours,

Letter No. 4

Dear Mr. Blank:

We cannot bring ourselves to believe that you will knowingly violate a business contract and by so doing affect your credit standing. And this is just what you are doing by letting your account with us remain unpaid. Already we have written you three letters about this matter, and you must admit that we have been very patient with you.

We have no desire to cause you any inconvenience or humiliation, which would naturally be a result of legal action or the repossession of your radio. But we must take definite steps to secure the payment of this overdue obligation unless we receive a check for $20.50 within the next five days.

Very truly yours,

[75]

Claim and Adjustment Letters

Principles of Claims

75a. Present the essential facts of the claims clearly, concisely, courteously, and in an orderly and logical manner. Effective claim letters are calm, tactful, fair, persuasive, and considerate.

b. Do not write angry, sarcastic, abusive, accusatory, or dictatorial letters. It is usually assumed that the error was unintentional.

c. For emphasis, state the claim in greater detail. Emphasis is not secured by anger or mere repetition of dissatisfaction.

d. Definite explanations are more effective than vague expressions of general dissatisfaction. To be explicit, give essential information, such as dates, invoice numbers, and file numbers.

e. Threaten withdrawal of trade only when the threat is seriously meant.

f. The claim letter may state specifically what adjustment is wanted, or it may leave the remedy to the adjuster.

Gentlemen:

On your statement of September 1, you show a balance for $6.35 dated May 28.

The merchandise that was received by your invoice #3232 of May 28 for $6.35 was returned to you.

We are enclosing a copy of our claim 24218 of June 13 for your convenience in checking.

Please credit this amount to our account.

Yours very truly,

FREDERICK & NELSON

The Structure of the Claim Letter

76. In its simplest form, the claim letter states the essential facts in chronological order with a request for prompt rectification. More complete claim letters usually contain the following elements:

(1) A specific explanation of the difficulty.

(2) A statement of the resulting inconvenience or trouble.

(3) An appeal to the seller's sense of fairness, pride, self-interest, or fear of loss of trade.

(4) A request for prompt explanation, investigation, or settlement of the difficulty.

Gentlemen:

On October 28 I ordered a twelve-volume history of World War I, expecting to use it for reference in preparing an address to be given on November 20.

The set did not reach me until two days later, the twenty-second, and I was, of course, disappointed and greatly inconvenienced by this tardy arrival.

Furthermore, upon looking through the books casually, I noticed that two of them have pages missing and another has several torn pages.

I am returning the three volumes to you today, by insured parcel post, and request that you please replace them with perfect copies.

Yours very truly,

Gentlemen:

The grapefruit that we ordered on January 2 and that you shipped on January 18 arrived yesterday in a very unsatisfactory condition. Fourteen of the boxes are spoiled so that we cannot use them for our holiday trade.

Naturally, we are inconvenienced and suffer some loss in not having at this time the amount of salable fruit ordered. Judging by our past experience with you, we feel sure that you will make us a refund or will send a new shipment immediately.

Yours very truly,

The Principles of Adjustments

77a. Answer the claim letter promptly. If an adjustment cannot be made at once, write a brief letter of acknowledgment expressing regret for the difficulty, with assurance of prompt action.

Dear Mr. Ogilvie:

This will acknowledge your letter of August 11 regarding the trouble you have experienced with tires of our manufacture.

We have built a reputation for fair dealing over a long period of years, and we can assure you that your claim will be investigated and that action will be taken consistent with the facts.

We have been making quality products for over 75 years, and we are anxious and willing to make proper adjustment in the event of failure caused by defective workmanship or material.

We are sending our District Manager in Buffalo a copy of your letter, together with a copy of this acknowledgment. He will have someone contact you, at the very earliest opportunity, to get the facts that prompted the statements made in your letter.

Feeling as you do about the matter, we are very glad you took the opportunity to write us.

Very truly yours,

THE B. F. GOODRICH COMPANY

b. The object of the adjustment letter is to settle the difficulty in a manner satisfactory to both house and customer and so retain the customer and build good will.

c. An effective adjustment letter is adapted to the claimant and shows consideration for his point of view. It is written in a spirit of service and fair treatment. It is a selling letter, inasmuch as it sells service, satisfaction, and good will. It is sincere, courteous, cheerfully phrased, and carefully planned. It explains the facts clearly, concisely, and fully. It convinces the claimant of the justness of the firm's decision.

d. The adjustment letter emphasizes the positive, constructive aspects of the problem. It does not emphasize the claimant's dissatisfaction or any other unpleasant aspect of the problem by needlessly restating the claim.

e. The adjustment letter assumes that the claimant is honest in his intentions. It does not try to put him in the wrong by suggesting, for instance, that he is ignorant or careless, nor does it try to force from him an admission of error. It is never angry, sarcastic, accusatory, or grudging. It avoids humor, flattery, and untruth. It does not express surprise at being notified of defects in goods or services. It gives information regarding the article or service pleasantly, but never with an attitude of instructing the customer or preaching to him.

Dear Mr. Muenzer:

We are glad you notified us promptly that some of your sheets were damaged in transit. It gives us a chance to clear up the difficulty without delay.

No doubt the error was made by one of the inspectors in the shipping department. We try to use every safeguard to prevent such an occurrence, but try as we do, there will be a slip once in a great while. Whenever this occurs, we are always glad to make things right as quickly as possible.

We have entered a re-place order for the fifty sheets. These will be sent not later than Monday of next week.

We are mighty sorry this happened, and in the future we shall do everything within our power to see that things are just as you want them.

Very truly yours,[1]

Granting Adjustments

78a. The adjustment is granted when the firm acknowledges responsibility because of defects in the goods, faults in service, delays in shipment, mistakes in filling orders, or similar errors.

b. In the letter granting the adjustment, frankly admit the error and assure the customer that precautions have been taken to avoid a repetition of the error. Make the letter cheerful and express regret for the inconvenience caused the customer. It is not necessary to apologize, to defend yourself, or to be profuse in expressing regret (such an attitude may imply intentional offense).

c. Elements and structure of the letter.

Opening: Get on common ground with the claimant. Make contact by thanking him for bringing the claim to your attention or by an expres-

[1] From *Making Letters Talk Business*, American Rolling Mill Co.

sion of agreement with him, of sympathy with him, or of regret for the inconvenience caused him.

Adjustment: Grant the customer's claim.

Explanation: Explain the facts of the claim, the cause of the difficulty, or the results of the investigation.

Close: Close the letter with assurance of future satisfaction, with a reselling talk, or with an expression of appreciation of the opportunity to correct the difficulty.

Note: The expression of regret may occur in the opening, in the explanation, or in the close.

d. The letter may be constructed according to various plans:

(1)

Dear Mr. Mound:

Regret: We regret very much to hear of the damage caused by the punctured can of Collodion, to which you referred in your letter of October 15.

Adjustment: On October 27 we sent you by express another can of Collodion and new cartons to replace those that were damaged.

Reassurance: We thank you for telling us about it, as this experience will prompt us to use greater care in future shipments.

Very truly yours,[2]

(2)

Dear Mr. Drake:

Adjustment: We are shipping X and Y to replace the goods mentioned in your letter of May 9.

[2] From *Writing Kodak Letters*, Eastman Kodak Company.

Explanation and regret: The error in the original shipment was made because the numbers in your order did not correspond with the goods you wanted. We are sorry that this has inconvenienced you.

Assurance of satisfaction: If you cannot use the A and B, of course we should like to have you return them at our expense for credit.

Very truly yours,[3]

(3)

Dear Mrs. Harris:

Admission of fault: We wish you to know that we appreciate your courtesy in writing to us of your dissatisfaction with your last transaction in our Beauty Parlor.

Adjustment: It is a pleasure to make full adjustment and to credit your account.

Explanation and regret: The manager of our Beauty Parlor, Mrs. Hopkins, and the operator, Miss Frane, both regret very much that the work did not please you, and if you should care to have them do so, they would be very glad to give you further attention.

Appreciation and sales talk: We thank you for the patronage you have extended to us and wish you to know that we value your friendship highly. We are always anxious to make every transaction satisfactory, and hope you will always inform us, as you did this time, if things are otherwise.

Very truly yours,

FRASER-PATERSON CO.

Refusing Adjustments

79a. When the claim is unfair or the buyer is to blame, the adjustment is refused.

[3] From *Writing Kodak Letters*, Eastman Kodak Company.

b. In refusing adjustments, state the essential facts in a logical, businesslike way so as to appeal to the customer's sense of fairness and retain his good will.

c. Clear yourself of blame, but do not throw the blame on the customer.

d. Consider the reader's point of view and make him satisfied with the decision.

e. Sometimes, it will be necessary to indicate that out of fairness to all your customers no exception can justly be made.

f. Structure of the letter.

Common ground and favorable contact: Get on common ground with the claimant; make a favorable contact. Put something pleasant first: agree with him in some way, express regret for the inconvenience caused him, thank him for bringing the claim to your attention, or sympathize with his point of view. Emphasize those aspects of the problem upon which buyer and seller agree.

Explanation: Give a logical and persuasive explanation of the facts of the claim, the cause of the difficulty, the results of the investigation, or the reasons for the action proposed. Prepare the claimant's mind to be receptive of the refusal.

Refusal: State the action proposed by the house. It may be helpful to tie this in with a fair and persuasive statement of the firm's adjustment policy.

Close: Induce the claimant to accept the decision. Insert a short sales talk. Imply continuance of the customer's good will.

[79]

Gentlemen:

Opening: We wish that we could accept the merchandise that you would like to close out of your stock, as suggested in your letter of October 12.

Explanation: If we knew of outlets for these goods, we should be glad to dispose of them for you.

Refusal: Even though they are but slightly shopworn, you will appreciate the fact that they cannot be sold for new, and consequently they would be valueless for our distribution.

Close: Please remember that we always try to coöperate with our dealers. In this particular case, we believe that you will understand our position.

Very truly yours,[4]

Dear Mr. Dealer:

Opening: We can furnish Mr. Barker a new BALANCE holder for his LIFETIME pen and still use the same point.

Explanation: Please explain to Mr. Barker that the job is like jacking up the motor in his car and running a new chassis under it. This new BALANCE "chassis" for the LIFETIME will cost $4 in jade or jet black, and $5 for black and pearl.

Refusal: We're confident that Mr. Barker won't expect us to do all this remodeling for nothing, but we wanted to make sure. We could just wash and polish that old "car," place it in perfect running condition, and not charge a dime for the work.

[4] From *Writing Kodak Letters*, Eastman Kodak Company.

Close: However, we would really rather have Mr. Barker use a BALANCED LIFETIME. Please see whether it's all right.

Very truly yours,

W. A. SHEAFFER PEN CO.

Other Adjustments

80a. Third party at fault. If the error is due to a third party or to some unavoidable accident, the letter expresses regret, indicates where the responsibility lies, and, if possible, offers help or suggests a remedy. This letter may contain the following points:

1. An expression of sympathy or regret.
2. An explanation of the facts.
3. An offer of help or of such adjustment as the situation demands.
4. The assurance that future treatment will be more satisfactory.

Dear Mr. Wallace:

Immediately upon receipt of your telegram of June 14, which came this morning, we began to trace the missing samples of enameling sheets.

The samples left our factory on the eleventh and should have been delivered to you on the fourteenth without fail. We have asked the express company to trace the shipment immediately.

If you do not receive the samples within a day or two, please let us know and we will start another shipment. We know you will like this material and we are anxious to get it to you.

Very truly yours,[5]

[5] From *Making Letters Talk Business*, The American Rolling Mill Co.

[80]

Dear Sir:

We are very sorry to know from your letter of March 14 that the mahogany desk you ordered as a birthday gift for your son arrived so badly marred that you cannot accept it.

As the Chicago, Milwaukee and St. Paul Railroad gave us a receipt acknowledging that the desk was received perfectly crated, it must have been damaged in transit. Although our responsibility ends when the railroad has accepted the desk, we know how much you are interested in this beautiful and useful gift for your son. We are, therefore, sending you today, by prepaid express, another desk, exactly like the one you ordered. It should reach you promptly.

If you will please telephone the express company to make a special delivery immediately upon the arrival of the desk at their receiving station, you should have the desk not later than the day of your son's birthday.

Please leave the damaged desk in the hands of the railroad. We shall enter a claim with them so that you will not be troubled further.

We thank you for writing promptly, and assure you that our only desire is that you receive the desk promptly and in perfect condition.

Very truly yours,[6]

b. Both parties at fault. When both parties are at fault, a compromise may be proposed to the customer.

Dear Mrs. Studer:

We wish you to know that we appreciate very much your courtesy in writing to us of your dissatisfaction with your magazine subscription contract.

We are always anxious to make every transaction satisfactory and want you to inform us, as you did in this case, if things are otherwise. With a company such as ours,

[6] From A. C. Babenroth, *Modern Business English*. New York: Prentice-Hall, Inc.

which represents a number of publishers all over the country, it is necessary that the subscriber notify us of change of address sixty days ahead. Through a mistake of one of our clerks, your first two notices of change of address went astray, and naturally you were quite annoyed when you failed to receive your magazines. However, since only two weeks elapsed between the sending of your first notice and your third, you were allowing us only thirty days in which to adjust the necessary changes in mailing address with four different publishers.

Now, we don't want you to do an injustice to yourself and to us by breaking your subscription contract. You undoubtedly enjoy these magazines, which, I believe, you said were favorites of yours; and the subscription price, as you know, is very low. So if you will mail us a check for $1.40 to pay for the magazines that you actually received, we will cancel your bill of $2.25, the amount called for by your contract.

That's fair enough, isn't it?

Very truly yours,

MACK MAGAZINES, INC.

c. **Adjustment as a matter of company policy.** The letter granting the claim in spite of the fact that the customer is at fault emphasizes the spirit of fair dealing and sells service. Although the letter is firm, it does not suggest that the claim is unjust or try to make the customer feel that he is receiving something to which he is not entitled.

Dear Mrs. Jones:

We want to thank you for your letter of frank criticism and for the generous attitude you have taken. We regret that we did not know of the matter sooner so that the proper adjustment could have been made promptly.

We feel sure that you will realize that, in an establishment such as this, we have to depend upon our employees to carry out the ideas and policies of the management. We safeguard ourselves by employing, as far as possible, people we believe to be capable of representing our store and its standards. Unfortunately, however, there are always some who utterly fail to do this, and in such cases we are always desirous of adjusting the matter as soon and as satisfactorily as possible.

We have credited you with twenty-five dollars and are instructing our delivery department to call for the dress. We are anxious to have you know also that we are doing this, not merely because you have made a claim, but because it is what we would naturally do in any case if the wishes of the management were carried out.

We again assure you that the patronage you have extended to us is appreciated very much, and we hope that our friendly relations may continue.

Yours very truly,

FRASER-PATERSON CO.

d. Small claims. When damage to the goods is slight, the letter can often induce the customer to keep the goods by the offer of some method of repair. Again, when the damage is not severe or when delay has decreased the value of the goods, the letter may offer a discount. However, such adjustments must satisfy the customer.

Dear Mrs. Kirk:

We are sorry to learn that the radio we recently sent you by express did not arrive in good condition. The small scratch on the side of the cabinet was probably caused by carelessness in packing.

However, the finish on Cleartone Radios has always been of such fine quality that a small scratch such as this is not likely to prove either serious or permanent if you follow our suggestions. Clean the surface thoroughly with the liquid in the red bottle which we are sending you. Then, after it is dry, apply the stain in the blue bottle, allow the stain to dry, and then rub the surface briskly with a dry cloth. We are confident that the scratch will entirely disappear and that the finish will be as good as when the cabinet left the factory.

We want you to be satisfied. If you are not pleased with the result, do not hesitate to write us again.

Very truly yours,

CLEARTONE RADIOS, INC.

e. **Unjustified discounts.** When the customer takes discounts to which he is not entitled, point out clearly the reason for insistence on a full remittance.

Dear Mr. Wightman:

Many thanks for the $675, which came in this morning.

It is evident that you are not quite clear as to the matter of cash discount, which is allowed on bills paid within 30 days after the invoice is rendered. Since your payment is 15 days overdue, we have passed the $675 to your credit, leaving a balance of $75, the amount deducted as discount. We feel sure, however, that you will now gladly send us your check for this balance.

You realize that only by the practice of prompt payment are we able to discount our own bills and pass on to our customers the benefit of the lowest possible price. Then, too, we treat all customers alike by maintaining our plan of settlement. Cash discount is really a desirable saving; and in the future you will, no doubt, get much benefit by taking advantage of this economy.

Yours very truly,[7]

f. **Asking the customer to state the adjustment.** If the customer does not wish to accept the proposed adjustment, the firm sometimes asks him to state what he thinks is a fair adjustment.

[7] From *Making Letters Talk Business*, The American Rolling Mill Co.

Dear Mrs. Bayley:

We appreciate your courtesy in answering our recent letter, and we thank you for your frank expression of criticism.

It is certainly most annoying to learn that something one has depended upon is not right, and we do not wonder that you were disappointed to find that the blouse you purchased here was not satisfactory. We realize that we cannot make up for the inconvenience you experienced, but we assure you that we shall be very glad to make any adjustment that would be acceptable to you in the matter of the blouse. Please ask for Mrs. Marshal on the third floor.

We value the friendship of our customers as our greatest asset, and endeavor at all times to give them the best within our power.

It is a pleasure to be of service to you at any time.

Very truly yours,

FRASER-PATERSON CO.

g. **Explanation of the facts.** When the customer makes a complaint about some policy or practice of the house, the adjustment letter explains the facts in such a way as to readjust the customer's attitude of mind.

Dear Mr. Mellon:

Your frank letter was referred to me, and despite your positive request that no letter of apology be written, I am writing you this letter, which, however, is to be a letter of thanks rather than an apology.

Once in a while, I read a report or a claim in which one of our customers has (as in this instance) a real, honest-to-goodness reason for thinking that Smith, Jones and Company do not know how to fill an order correctly. I question whether, if I were you, I should have written as considerately as you did. I sometimes wonder, when such a report comes to me, why some of our customers don't take their business elsewhere without letting us know their grievance. That is why Smith, Jones and Company should thank you for letting us know where we have fallen down in connection with your business.

Your order was filled on December 18. During those few days prior to Christmas, we received more than double the usual amount of business. We had nearly 6,000 employees, some of whom had been brought into our store for temporary work last fall and had not become as thoroughly trained as our regular employees. With the great increase in volume of orders, coupled with our desire to get every last order to our customers for Christmas, and with a percentage of comparatively inexperienced employees, the ordinarily careful supervision and inspection of orders was probably relaxed. The management of a business such as ours, therefore, has to depend, to some extent, on the letters that come from customers; and it is for this reason that I welcome yours, although it is a good deal like taking medicine to do so.

We want an opportunity to prove to you that Smith, Jones and Company can and do handle orders correctly; and since we have had so much misfortune in connection with your orders, I am going to ask that, in the event you do decide to give us an opportunity of showing you that your experience is not typical, you send your next few orders to me personally, so that I may have them checked and satisfy myself that you are not going to be caused further inconvenience.

This is done because I am sure you are convinced that in buying from us you do save money and that your sole reason for discontinuing your dealings with us is that we have made mistakes in recent orders.

Very truly yours,

SMITH, JONES AND COMPANY

Dear Mrs. Rich:

Thank you for commenting on the questionnaire that you found in your room when you visited us recently.

For a weary traveler, looking forward to a comfortable room and bed, I realize that a five-hour wait is disappointing, particularly after you had made your reservation in advance. Your experience is regretted the more keenly because the comments on your questionnaire indicate that this was your first visit to the Roosevelt.

Every now and then plans do not carry. When a guest tells us he is leaving at three o'clock and then is unavoidably detained until eight or nine o'clock, the incoming guest who has been assigned to that room is inconvenienced.

I want to thank you for not protesting more vigorously; I somehow feel that you understand how such a delay might occur in these days. My only hope is that you will be willing to overlook what was an uncomfortable experience and will return to the Roosevelt again and again.

Very truly yours,

HOTEL ROOSEVELT

Inviting Claims

81. Firms often invite just claims and justified complaints in an attempt to reopen inactive accounts. Make the letter inviting a claim or a complaint personal, sincere, and appropriate; make the spirit of the letter one of cheerful coöperation.

Dear Miss Hazen:

This is a different kind of letter—a "halfway" letter:

This half is ours.	This half is yours.
You haven't used your charge account here for several months. There must be some reason why, and that's your side of the story, the side we want to get.	

Losing a good customer is like losing a friend.

We couldn't let either drift away in silence—without finding out if we've been at fault.

That's our side.

Will you meet us halfway?

The other half of this "halfway" letter is yours. If you will use it to tell us just what's wrong, we'll consider it a personal favor.

Sincerely,

President

LIPMAN WOLFE & CO. Signature____________

Dear Miss Wald:

If one of these days you should discover that a mighty good friend of yours had suddenly stopped visiting you without apparent cause, you would want to know why, wouldn't you? You will readily understand, then, our great concern at seeing by our ledgers that you have apparently not been visiting us.

Although we have always done the very best we could to give you the greatest courtesy and service, being human, we may possibly have done something that did not entirely meet with your satisfaction. If this is so, won't you either write me or come in and tell me about it? You can rest assured that we will make things right, whatever the trouble was, for we shall not feel that we are a success until your account bears evidence that you are again one of our regular patrons.

Yours very truly,

LIPMAN WOLFE & CO.

Common Errors

82a. The adjustment letter errs if it expresses surprise at the claim or complaint, makes exaggerated statements, argues with the customer, or indulges in over-explanation.

Wrong:

We are surprised that you misunderstood our letter of the tenth. We surely tried to make matters clear.

If the difficulty you complain of was caused by a faulty manufacture, it would certainly seem that we would get complaints from other users.

Your statement that it is the policy of the company never to admit they are wrong is not well taken, because if we find anything wrong with our goods, we are perfectly willing to admit it.

Just a glance at our bill is enough to reveal the fact that we grant cash discount only when the payment is made within thirty days after the bill is rendered.

We cannot understand your attitude about this.

b. Do not use such words and phrases as the following in adjustment letters:

cannot understand
at a loss
never happen again
complaint
you assert (state, say, claim)
we hope (trust) this will be satisfactory
if this is not satisfactory, let us know
to set you right
all we ask is fairness
hoping, trusting, thanking, *and all other participial endings*

Sales Letters

The Analysis of the Product and of the Prospect

83a. Analysis of the product.

(1) The first step in the construction of a sales letter is to secure a thorough and confident knowledge of the product or service to be sold through the medium of the sales letter. The writer should be familiar with the following:

(a) *The Raw Materials.* Kind, source of supply, quality, cost, quantity available. Such information may be obtained through first-hand observation or experience, talks with purchasing agents or other qualified officials, or reference books (commercial geographies and encyclopedias), scientific treatises, or specialized studies.

(b) *The Manufacturing Processes.* Factory methods and processes (learned in the factory or through talks with managers, foremen, mechanics, and other qualified personnel), machinery and equipment, plant capacity, cost, labor-saving and time-saving devices, production time, standards of workmanship, supervision, sanitation and purity.

(c) *The Finished Product.* Quality, uses, design, service, price, methods of distribution.

(2) Analysis of these basic data will reveal the individualizing features that distinguish your article

from competing products. Your product, for example, may have the advantage in price, design, or service. These differentiating features suggest what talking points it is desirable to stress in the sales letter.

(3) Information about the product or service may also be secured from experiments and tests and from the experiences of users, salesmen, and dealers.

(4) It is desirable also to have a knowledge of the organization and operation of the company, its history, its policies, and its various departments, especially sales, credit, collection, adjustment, receiving, and shipping.

b. Analysis of the prospect or market.

(1) The second step in the construction of a sales letter is to secure a thorough and confident knowledge of the prospect (the market) to whom the product or service is to be sold, so that effective adaptation may be employed in choosing the selling appeal, the style, and the tone of the letter.

(2) It is essential to know something about the prospective retail customer's buying habits, buying power, needs and desires, economic, social, and educational level, and type of community. In selling to a dealer, it is helpful to know something about the character and size of his business, his requirements, his capital or finances, his location, his policies, his competition, local business conditions, his methods, his credit standing, the important problems in his business, his personal characteristics, his ambitions, hobbies, and manner of living, his office and home environment, and the opportune time for letters to arrive.

(3) **Such information may be secured from professional market analyses by marketing specialists. Information may also be secured from such various sources as questionnaires, talks with salesmen, customers, and acquaintances, tests made to sound out a list, records of former mailings, the customer's past correspondence on file, the selling experience of the firm, special trade investigations, governmental sources, rating books, books on the trade, and trade magazines.**

The Central Selling Point and Supporting Material

84a. The central selling point.

(1) **The central selling point is the outstanding quality or utility of a product or service that influences the reader to buy. Although a product or service may possess several distinguishing features, the letter should concentrate on one.**

Suppose we are writing a letter selling the Writewell Fountain Pen. An analysis of this pen discloses the following distinguishing features:

National advertising.
Lifetime guarantee.
Perfect balance.
Economy of operation.
Standard price.
Proper color cycle.
Iridium point.

The letter, then, concentrates on just one of these distinguishing features—BALANCE. Thus, Balance becomes the central selling point of this particular letter.

However, subsequent letters may concentrate on any one of the other outstanding features—

guarantee, iridium point, or economy—and make it the central selling point of that particular letter.

(2) **Discover the central selling point by analyzing the differentiating features of the product or service in relation to the needs and desires of the reader. The one feature that best satisfies his needs or that will best influence him to buy should form the basis of the letter as the central selling point.**

(3) **In advancing a reason why the customer should buy, the central selling point arouses in him a buying motive and thus leads to the sale of the product.**

b. The supporting material.

(1) **In choosing material to support the central selling point, select only those details that focus directly upon the central selling point.**

The central selling point is assumed to be the *balance* of the fountain pen.

Such details as the following may be selected as the supporting material:

A distinctive feature of the Writewell.
Feather touch.
Tireless writing.
Weightless reservoir, filling device, and cap.
Increased writing speed.
Flow sensitized to the lightest stroke.

(2) **The nature of the product determines the choice of the supporting material.** If the product is a necessity and satisfies a need, make the letter appeal to the judgment of the prospect and include in the supporting material substantial, verifiable data, such as facts and figures. If the product is a

luxury or satisfies merely a desire, make the appeal emotional and include in the supporting material details that have color, atmosphere, and suggestiveness.

The Structure of the Sales Letter

85. A complete sales letter contains four essential elements or steps.[1] In practice these four headings shade into each other and are not always sharply outlined:

(*a*) Favorable attention.
(*b*) Desire.
(*c*) Conviction.
(*d*) Action.

Dear Mr. Boyle:

Attention: Relieve your wife of fire-tending drudgery. Free her from the continual nuisance and work of trying to regulate the home temperature by hand.

Desire: When she is out for the day, let her mind be at ease because she knows that during her absence the heating plant will be AUTOMATICALLY and safely regulated, and that it will keep the house steadily at just the temperature desired.

Conviction: The Minneapolis-Honeywell Heat Regulator will do the work for her, with a minimum amount of supervision on her part.

You needn't get up early in a cold house to start the fire. The Regulator will do it for you, automatically, while you sleep. Then, after dressing and breakfasting comfortably in a warm house, put some coal on the fire—less coal than you do now, for the Regulator, by preventing overheating, saves considerable fuel—and for the rest of the day you can forget your heating plant.

[1] Some authorities interpret (*b*) as Interest and (*c*) as Desire and Conviction.

Action: Phone the automatic temperature control expert now. You'll find his name in the telephone book, listed under "Minneapolis-Honeywell." Have him call today!

Very truly yours,

MINNEAPOLIS-HONEYWELL
REGULATOR CO.

Beginnings

86a. The purpose of the beginning is to win the reader's attention and interest, excite his curiosity, and so induce him to read farther. The opening establishes contact through an appeal to his needs, self-interest, and desires. The writer must be careful that the attention-getter produces the right emotional reaction and has the *you* attitude.

b. Effective beginnings.

(1) Timely news items or current events and references to seasonal activities and holidays.

The recent investigation of present water conditions in New Jersey discloses the fact that many of the sources of supply are highly corrosive in their effects on pipe materials.

Between now and fall, you'll be planning for your share of the school opening business.

It seems to be spring! Tiny yellow daffodils poke their heads up out of the cool, moist earth. The days are becoming warm and inviting. And along with spring days comes the desire for new clothes.

(2) Significant fact.

You CAN have warm rooms to dress in.

Ninety-six per cent of all players in Hollywood use Max Factor's Make-Up.

You can double your income without increasing your investment, provided you can turn your stock twice as often.

Right now, ten thousand youngsters are catching cold in chilly, drafty rooms.

More than 2,000,000 Everdur bolts have been placed in transmission line service during the past three years. To date, not a single one of these bolts has been reported as failing.

(3) Pertinent question.

Step into your employer's office tomorrow and demand a one hundred per cent increase in your salary. Would you get it?

Have you ever stood at your door and wondered what makes those "cross-the-street customers" your competitor's rather than your own?

Where is there a name in the tire industry equal to the name Silvertown?

(4) *IF* opening.

If "Smoker's Fag" is beginning to get you, you can correct it by doing one simple thing.

If your wife should put her heart on paper, is *this* what she would say to you?

If you want amazing performance at low cost—hear the new Philco.

(5) Split opening.

When you can't quite remember where you saw that store—

Turn to your Classified Telephone Directory.

Large estates, yachts, glorious round-the-world trips—luxuries most of your customers will probably never enjoy—

But there is one luxury within the reach of them all.

(6) **Anecdote, story, or human interest reference.**

A small boy had been given enough money to go to the circus. But he came home very much disappointed. He had not got into the big tent, having spent his money on red lemonade, hot dogs, and side shows.

I sometimes wonder if the merchant who complains of not getting value received for the money he spends on advertising is not like the little boy who failed to get into the circus.

(7) **Command.**

Tune in on all the world!

Give your throat a holiday with Camels.

Fight your cold, asleep or awake.

(8) **Quotation from prominent or recognized authority (a miniature testimonial).**

"The common cold probably causes more loss in dollars and cents," says Dr. Frederic Damrau, "than any other disease."

(9) **Reference to some friend or acquaintance.**

Walter Long pays the rent, heat, light, postage, and janitor service costs of his automobile business out of the profit he makes in the tire business.

Right in your own neighborhood, only two miles from your place, your neighbor, Henry Adams, is putting in two Armco Ingot Iron culverts.

c. **Weak beginnings:**

(1) **Trite, colorless, or timorous openings expressed in the language of trade announcements.**

We are pleased to advise you that we are now sole agents for Syracuse China.

We have just received a new automatic toaster known as the Toastero.

A quantity of fine bath powder in which you may be interested is now on sale at our cosmetic department.

(2) **Negative openings, such as apologies and unpleasant and painful suggestions** (except in articles the chief value of which is to protect the reader from disagreeable experiences; here the "scare" opening may effectively be used).

Will you be a burden on your relatives at sixty?

Why be anemic and scrawny when Vitalized Yeast will put firm flesh on your bones?

Although you may not be interested in more insurance, read this letter anyway.

We don't like to bother you—but we have a real message for you.

Do you selfishly deny your wife the pleasure of afternoon bridge parties because you need the family car in your business?

(3) **Irrelevant openings.**

You know, Mr. Wheeler, you can feed a horse sawdust and it will fill him up, but he won't remain a good horse very long if you do.

Next to your own personal affairs, your store is one of the most important things in the world.

(4) **Indirect and vague openings or weak generalities.**

Plenty of stores in this country today are serving just as many customers as in boom times. But their gross sales and profits are down. Why? Because the average sale per customer has sunk far below the previous average.

(5) **Fake, deceptive, or "clever" openings.**

How would you like to make $1,000,000 in three

weeks? Well, the only way you can do it is to set up a mint of your own. But here, we've got a real proposition for you.

(6) ***We* openings.**

We are sure that you would like to have one of these beautiful, indestructible La Sonia necklaces.

We believe we have the finest radio ever offered to the American public.

d. Good beginnings must be brief, original, and appropriate; direct, relevant, and positive; specific and concrete; expressed in simple and familiar diction and written in the *you* attitude.

Desire and Appeals

87a. The creation of desire involves (1) selecting the central selling point and the corresponding instinct, need, desire, or buying motive that the product satisfies and (2) making the reader aware of his need or desire by describing the article physically (reason-why appeal) or emotionally (short-circuit appeal).

b. The reason-why appeal is a mental appeal to the reason or the judgment of the reader. It seeks to influence him to buy through the presentation of arguments or data that will convince him of the superiority of the product in satisfying his needs. Physical description is concerned with factual details, such as size, shape, color, weight, texture, materials, operation, and construction. It should be brief and suggestive. The detailed work is done by enclosures.

Palmolive Shaving Cream makes your shave easier by multiplying itself in lather 250 times, by softening the beard in one minute, and by maintaining its creamy fullness for ten minutes on the face.

The price of the Filer is $69. That's fair enough if you look at it in this way. There are thousands of Uarco registers now in use that are more than twenty years old. Figuring the cost of the Filer over that period of time, it costs about *a penny a day.*

Look at the heavy-duty understructure, the massive double-drop frame, the patented slayed under-and-longer springs, the solid-unit, rattle-proof steel body.

c. **The short-circuit appeal is an appeal to the emotions, the desires, and the imagination of the reader.** By presenting a product persuasively, it arouses a desire in the prospect, and then induces him to buy through connecting the satisfaction of the desire with the use of the product. Emotional description suggests the feelings, sensations, pleasure, or satisfaction that the article will give. It makes a concrete appeal to the senses and tries to stir the emotions. It visualizes the article in terms of convenience, pride, comfort, and so forth.

What you do get is marvellously tender ham, every bit of it eatable. This ham comes to your table with no waste and none of that terrific shrinkage you pay for when you cook ham.

There is no more fumbling with buttons, for a quick pull makes you snug and warm against wind and sleet.

The house is warm and pleasant by the time you get up—no one has touched the heating plant! Instead, an extra hour of undisturbed sleep helps start the day right.

There's a frosty sparkle in the depths of Canada Dry, a glint of gold in its color, and an exhilaration in its taste that fits right in with the occasion.

Ingram's is the first shaving cream planned to take the nicking sting out of your morning shave and to leave a clear cheek and a cool skin when the job is finished. Its three special ingredients cool and soothe your face from the moment you put on the lather.

[87]

This book is like a pocket newsreel of all the things you'll enjoy most . . . golf, riding, tennis, and every other sport . . . sparkling blue waters for sails to pleasure-islands near the Pacific's sandy shore . . . gay night life in Hollywood, where you'll mingle with the stars . . . the sun-drenched winter desert . . . forested mountains and crystal lakes.

Each chocolate is a masterpiece whether its center be a nut-studded nougat or a juicy cherry; a plain fruit-flavored cream or a date stuffed with a nut; whether it be a tangy jelly or a brittle taffy.

d. The reason-why appeal is better adapted to satisfying needs.

Gentlemen:

On the front of the enclosed bulletin is pictured the most popular model in our line of industrial diesel-electric locomotives—the 45-tonner.

In 1940, the first full year it was available, 14 were placed in service; last year nearly 100 were delivered, and as of January 1, 1950, more than 300 were at work—taking LESS time to do MORE hauling and switching work in the steel, oil, mining, shipbuilding, rock products, and many other industries.

At a shipyard in North Carolina, for example, six of these 45-tonners are handling the heavy switching promptly and economically. They turn in a total of 128 hours of work every day—a daily average of 21 hours per locomotive. Much of this work is done around sharp curves and up 800 feet of 2 per cent grade on the lead track. The yard's records show that each diesel-electric uses only three gallons of fuel an hour while it's working, and unlike steam locomotives, there's no fuel used while standing by.

Whether you need modern motive power for switching or haulage, there's a standard, performance-proved G-E diesel-electric that will give you unusually high availability and low operating cost. We'll be glad to survey your operation to help you determine the right selection of motive power for your particular work.

Very truly yours,

GENERAL ELECTRIC COMPANY

e. The short-circuit appeal is better suited to satisfying desires and longings of a more personal nature.

Dear Mr. Martin:

Romantic Curaçao is calling you! Come to this vacation land set in a world apart from the busy routines of the workaday world. A charming bit of old Holland transplanted to a tiny, sundrenched isle in the wide, blue Caribbean!

Swim in the warm Caribbean waters, or stretch out on the gleaming white sand and bask in the golden warmth of the tropic sun while the foaming, crashing breakers roll in along the shore. Take your family out the palm-lined shore road to Newport, the queen of resorts. Eat the most famous Dutch meals in the western world at the Hotel Wilhemina, where the everyday cuisine is built upon the secret recipes of centuries of famous Dutch cooks. Tour through the huge, new C.P.I.M. oil refinery, which covers the surrounding green hills behind the city and whose tall, thin stacks and short, round storage tanks lend a modern note in contrast to the Old World air of Curaçao. See the quaint Dutch-style houses of Willemstad, bright with vivid blues, reds, greens, and yellows, exotic with their typical Dutch half-doors, red tile roofs, and pots of gaily colored geraniums.

Look through the enclosed folder. It shows you only a fraction of the myriad attractions of Curaçao. Curaçao can be reached by both airplane and steamer. For your convenience we have compiled a combination price list and flight and sailing list of the well-known inter-Caribbean travel lines.

Do not put off your well-deserved winter vacation another day! For accommodations and reservations check the enclosed card and mail it to the Netherlands Information Bureau, Mills Building, 22 Bush Street, San Francisco 5, California.

Remember—Curaçao is calling you!

Very truly yours,

NETHERLANDS INFORMATION BUREAU

The Buying Motives

88. The buying motive is the instinct or desire that prompts the purchaser to buy a product. A selling point or appeal is the quality or use of a product that stimulates a buying motive in the purchaser. Consumers buy products when the selling point of the letter appeals to one of these buying motives.[2]

Positive appeals:

activity (physical or mental)
acquisitiveness
ambition
amusement
appetite
approval of others
beauty
cleanliness
comfort (bodily or mental)
competition
constructiveness
convenience
coolness
courtesy
curiosity
desire for gain
devotion to others
domesticity
durability
duty
economy
efficiency
endurance
exclusiveness
friendliness
gregariousness
group loyalty
health
home comfort
hope
hospitality
hunger
imitation
leisure
love
love of home and family
managing others
manipulation

[2] Buying behavior is, of course, influenced not only by the buying motive, but also by economic and social environment, experience and education, special training, and individual and group interests.

maternal instinct
orderliness
ornamentation
parental love
personal appearance
play
pleasure
possession
pride
profits
prosperity
protection of others
purity
quality
relaxation
rest (sleep)
safety
self-esteem
self-indulgence
self-preservation
sex attraction
shyness and modesty
social ambition
style
sympathy
taste
thrift
vanity
warmth
work
worship

Negative appeals (generally to be avoided; "scare" appeals are, however, effectively used with products or services whose purpose is to protect the customer against undesirable contingencies):

caution
despair
dread
failure
fear
loss

In the following specimen are appeals to the motives of parental love, thrift, coöperation, and protection:

Dear Mr. Du Maurier:

Do you know the greatest gift you can give your son? It isn't a bike or a pitcher's glove, even though he may think so at the moment. And it isn't the price of a movie, either.

When you sit down and really think about it, you'll agree when I say the greatest gift you can give your boy is an understanding of the word *thrift.* Thrift is sometimes unattractive. Often the youngster feels it means giving up something he wants badly for something he just doesn't understand.

If so, he—and you, too—will be interested in Penn Mutual's Father and Son Plan. Here's something your son *can* understand—something he'll be glad to work for—a real partnership with Dad!

The details of this plan are interestingly unfolded in a new booklet called "That Boy of Yours." We want to send it to you because we know both he and you will be fascinated with the "behind-the-scenes" workings of this grand partnership plan.

This plan is much more than insurance as you and I knew it way back. If you make this "deal" with your son, you'll be doing something for him that nothing else, much less money, can ever buy. You'll make a MAN of him.

Send for the booklet. Read it. Let him read it. Then watch the reaction. There's no obligation—simply mail the post-free card.

Yours very truly,

THE PENN MUTUAL LIFE
INSURANCE COMPANY

Conviction and Evidence

89a. By the use of evidence, convince the reader that your statements are true and that the product meets his needs or desires.

(1) **Facts and figures.** Facts and figures must be definite and verifiable. They should be presented in a concrete, specific manner and in a form adapted to the understanding of the reader. Pictorial devices, photographs, or graphs may be used.

Bronze screens cannot rust. They withstand weather and wear. They remain taut and firm, new-like for years. *And they are not expensive.* Bronze screen cloth retails for only fifty cents to seventy-five cents more a window than screening that rusts—a small amount for lasting value without upkeep cost.

For with one motion, Addressograph does the work of 50 to 100 motions—10 to 50 times faster—and absolutely without error.

(2) **Testimonials.** Testimonials are effective if the user is favorably known and is unprejudiced. Usually, they should be put in the enclosure or reproduced in facsimile.

Over at Springfield, Ohio, the Armstrong Manufacturing Company has been making tubs and pails for several years. They were making them from galvanized steel, but they changed to Armco Ingot Iron.

Why? Let Mr. Armstrong tell you in his own words:

"We now use Armco Ingot Iron Galvanized Sheets after having given them a thorough test to determine the workability and welding qualities of the metal. The iron forms easily, and the coating does not peel. Our loss, caused by the poor working qualities of steel, has decreased ten per cent since we changed to Armco Ingot Iron Galvanized Sheets. In addition, our tubs and pails find a more ready market, because Armco Ingot Iron is so well and favorably known."

(3) **References.** References to satisfied customers are convincing when the list is impressive not only for length, but also for quality.

General Motors, Goodyear, General Electric, Chrysler, Goodrich, Holland Furnace, General Tire, Sinclair, Atwater-Kent and their printers, among others, have already put Beckett Plater Finish Offset to work.

Henry Adams decided to use metal culverts after he had thoroughly investigated other kinds. And he chose Armco Ingot Iron because he is convinced that it will give him the longest service.

(4) **Trial use.** Trial use convinces the reader that you have faith in your product, and appeals to the evidence of his own senses.

The first time you try Sanka Coffee, drink it at night. It won't keep you awake. Next morning you'll know, from actual experience, that you've discovered a delicious coffee that you can enjoy morning, noon, and night —without regret.

A week from today, after you have enjoyed seven cool Ingram shaves, get the economical regular size of Ingram's—more than enough for one hundred shaves.

(5) **Samples.** Samples make an appeal to the reader's own senses. They should arrive while the prospect's interest is still fresh and should be accompanied by printed instructions.

We want you to try Heinz Rice Flakes at our expense. So we'll send you a generous free trial package—enough for three delicious servings—free.

Let us send you samples of these sturdy, laboratory-proved Columbian Clasp envelopes for your heavier-than-letter mail.

(6) **Tests.** Tests make an appeal to the reader's own senses. They are of various kinds: (*a*) those made by the manufacturer, (*b*) those made by the consumer himself, and (*c*) those made by impartial, scientific testing laboratories.

This simple test can be made in any home refrigerator. Two hourglasses, one filled with Texaco and one with a poorly adapted motor oil, were frozen in a cake of ice. Texaco flowed freely at this low temperature. The other oil thickened like molasses.

Results count. Facts talk. A five-minute ride will tell you more than all the words in the world. Drive a new Plymouth and decide for yourself.

Try this dissolving test. Put one of the new curly Ivory Flakes in your hand. Pour a teaspoonful of warm water over it. Then another. Notice how the flake melts away first at the curly edges—then completely! In the wash basin, one swish dissolves the new Ivory Flakes instantly, even in lukewarm water—they can't flatten down on the fabric. No danger of soap spots.

(7) **Guarantees.** Guarantees are effective when the firm making the guarantee is known and respected. The language of the guarantee should show restraint.

All Sheaffer pens are guaranteed for life, and the Sheaffer Lifetime pen is guaranteed unconditionally against everything except loss for the life of the owner.

In fairness to yourself—check these questions before you buy. Only Frigidaire answers all of them in the way you want them answered. And only Frigidaire is backed by a three-year General Motors guarantee.

b. In presenting evidence, use statements that are specific and concrete and that appeal to the imagination of the reader. The evidence will be effective if the statements are conservative but confident.

In all, the advantages of permanent screens made of Anaconda Bronze Wire will be brought to the attention of more than 4,500,000 people.

The low first cost of Art Metal Transfer Cases dwindles to a vanishing point when you consider their long life and definite assurance of years of protection from fire, water, dust, dirt, and rodents.

c. Make references to enclosures vital and stimulating. Specific mention by page or section number is desirable.

You will find "Catalogues That Sell" good reading. We are sending it to you promptly, as you asked.

Sales executives in your kind of business usually find the suggestions on page four of particular interest. Why not turn to page four first? These ideas ought to be worth adopting right in your own company.

Closes or Clinchers

90a. Make the close of the sales letter stimulate the reader to one definite action.

Mail the enclosed coupon instructing our salesman to call on you.

Telephone Harrison 8765, and Mr. Burns will drivo out a new Buick so that you yourself may judge its excellence.

b. Effective closes:

(1) A courteous command or a persuasive suggestion.

Drop into the corner store and just say "Sunkist."

For the sake of the only eyes you will ever have, come in soon for a new examination.

Change over . . . over to Goodrich. Play safe.

It's waiting for you at the nearest drug store now!

Let us tell you how it can be done.

Simply indicate the dimensions of your roof on the enclosed stamped card.

(2) A definite, direct statement.

Every day you are without it is costing you money!

This is your chance to test yourself.

You owe it to yourself to let Mr. Bonson prove this to you.

It means assured profits for you.

(3) A restatement of the central selling point.

Any Sheaffer pen that you choose is guaranteed for a lifetime of satisfactory service.

You can afford to buy a tool of this kind that pays for itself in so short a time.

It relieves his inventory, helps balance his stock control, and means that less money is tied up in the pen department. The turnover is easier on Sheaffer's.

(4) A pertinent question.

Isn't a story like this worth investigating?

Won't you come in and see for yourself what comfort Autogarts can give?

(5) A pertinent condition.

And if, in the dead of night on Christmas Eve, you suddenly wake to the awful realization that you've missed someone, dash right down to Frank Nau's—we never close.

If you are handling a line that is hard to sell because it is unknown, it will pay you to get the complete story of the Goodrich franchise.

(6) An invitation (for letters not directly requesting orders).

This service is free to you, and the *Times* wants you to make use of it and to ask as many questions as you like as often as you like.

We'll be glad to show you our new spring suits and topcoats. And you'll be glad to see them.

c. The close will clinch the sale if the following principles are observed:

(1) There must be an inducement to immediate action: some advantage or premium for prompt response, limited supply, limited time offer, or advance in price.

Remember—the customary five per cent discount is applicable to your order. But we can hold this offer open to you only until April 15. So be prompt!

Just one thing you DON'T get—time to delay your decision. This offer is for immediate acceptance! Let me hear from you at once before the edition is sold out.

(2) **Action should be made easy.** Specific directions —what to do and how to do it—should be given, and action should be simplified by such devices as order blanks, return cards, and addressed, postage-paid envelopes.

Simply O. K. and return the enclosed card.

No postage is required. Just write your name and address and the name and address of your hardware jobber on the post card, and drop it into the nearest mail box.

(3) **The clincher must be positive.**

On your next trip go KAMPKOOK equipped.

A survey of your plans by the Minneapolis-Honeywell representative will assure you heating satisfaction.

(4) **The clincher must be adapted to the reader.**

Plan now to attend this summer school—it is an important step in reaching your goal.

Let our experienced engineers study your plans at no cost to you, and make recommendations that assure the utmost in economical, healthful heating.

d. Ineffective closes:

(1) **Stereotyped closes.**

Kindly advise us as to your needs.

Upon receipt of your remittance we will send you the Book of Marvels postpaid.

A telephone call from you will receive prompt attention.

We are hoping to hear from you soon and trust that you will place a substantial order with us.

Your money will be promptly refunded if you are not more than pleased.

DON'T DELAY. Send your name to us on the enclosed card TODAY!

(2) Participial closes.

Thanking you for past favors and trusting I may have the pleasure of serving you again.

Hoping that the writer may have the pleasure of your early acceptance.

Trusting in your future patronage and support.

(3) Discourteous commands.

Come into our store tomorrow. It doesn't cost you anything just to look around.

If you have any sense of true value, buy this radio.

We assure you that no intelligent person can do without this book. Get your copy today and prove to yourself that you are still mentally alive.

Drop whatever you are doing and mail this coupon right now.

(4) *We* closes.

We urge you to take advantage of this good offer.

We are positive that you will agree with us that this is the best radio on the market.

We carry a complete stock of all sizes and styles.

(5) Vague or general closes.

Parisian bath powders have a smooth quality of finesse and are sold at drug stores.

We are deeply repaid if we assist in making our city one of comfortable and attractive homes.

Fair golfers have fair clubs, but good golfers require more than good clubs. Theirs must be perfect.

(6) **Irrelevant closes.**

There's good weather ahead.

The results of certain basic innovations are astonishing in their effects on every phase of airplane travel—beauty, comfort, safety, strength, and most impressive of all—performance itself.

(7) **"Clever" or humorous closes.**

Of course we know when you get this information you will be so "hot and bothered" that you will rush right over to the Western Union and tell us all about it.

Birdies and our suits go together.

(8) **Closes asking a favor.**

Your reply would be a favor to us.

Will you please write to us?

We will appreciate your reading of the enclosure and boosting our sales volume by filling out and mailing the order blank.

We are anxious to establish Lexington Blankets. If you can, please favor us with an order.

e. **The stimulus to action completes the body of the letter. The complimentary close follows immediately.**

Our representative can prove to you that the Kerrigan System will prevent carelessness and put you on the road to greater prosperity.

Very truly yours,

f. **Negative clinchers.** Avoid negative suggestions in the clincher. Any statement arousing doubt in the reader's mind, making disagreeable suggestions, or setting up resistance, is negative and ineffective.

Why give us *no* as an answer?

I don't suppose that you will want to order now, but I thought I would call this offer to your attention.

Don't throw away this letter and dismiss the matter from your mind.

Are not these facts worth considering before you invest your money elsewhere?

g. Inverted clinchers. Do not insert material between the clincher and the complimentary close.

Inverted: Don't wait until tomorrow. Get your Clarion today. We guarantee you the finest thing in radio.

Correct: You will say it is the finest thing in radio. Get your Clarion today.

Inverted: May we send it? Returning the enclosed card obligates you in no way. It merely gives us the pleasure of sending you a booklet to look over at your leisure.

Correct: Returning the enclosed card obligates you in no way. It merely gives us the pleasure of sending you a booklet to look over at your leisure.

May we send it?

h. Divided clinchers. Never allow the reader choice of two or more actions.

Weak: We will greatly appreciate an opportunity to show this line to you at our store. However, if it is more convenient for you, we will gladly have one of our representatives get in touch with you.

Strong: May our representative call?

Weak: The next time you are in town let us show you the convenience and economy of the new Sweepsall. Or ask your neighbors about it.

Strong: Ask your neighbors about it.

Letters to Special Classes

Letters to Men

91a. Base letters to men on logic and conviction. Use the reason-why appeal. These letters try to relate the experiences common to men in general to the particular reader.

Dear Mr. Smith:

When you build your home, it will pay you to remember that cheap materials are not necessarily economical materials. Low first cost seldom buys durability, but often leads to expensive upkeep or replacement.

This is particularly true when metals that rust are used for service where water and moisture are encountered. Anaconda metals cannot rust and are by far the most economical to use. Copper sheet metal work, brass pipe plumbing, copper or Everdur hot water tanks, bronze screens, and solid brass or bronze hardware pay for their slightly higher first cost many times over by the repair and replacement expense they save.

The attached sheet points out those instances in which economy dictates the use of rust-proof metals. For further information, send the enclosed card for the booklet described at the left.

Very truly yours,

THE AMERICAN BRASS COMPANY

b. Appeal to the motives of ambition, the desire for success, power, responsibility, recognition or honor, increased income, betterment of position, efficiency, economy, or saving of time and labor.

[92]

Dear Mr. White:

Step into your employer's office tomorrow and demand 100 per cent increase in your salary. Will you get it?

Could you step out to some other firm and get a job paying twice your present salary? Probably not, else you would do it, of course.

Yet this is exactly what LaSalle-trained men are doing every day. Not a day passes that we do not receive a number of letters telling of promotions and increases from 10 to 500 per cent.

Just to substantiate this statement, I am sending you a circular which contains the names of over a thousand LaSalle members who have voluntarily reported actual increases in salary during a period of six months. I have classified these by states, giving actual names, the actual dollars or percentage of increased earnings, and the promotions as the result of LaSalle training. Perhaps you may know, or know of, some of these people.

You can number yourself among these successful men with a little of your spare time spent in preparation for an expert's position. Action will enable you to win greater rewards. Take the first step—send in your application for membership today.

Very truly yours,

LASALLE EXTENSION UNIVERSITY

Letters to Women

92a. Letters to women should have an attractive appearance reflecting taste and refinement. The letters may be given a feminine touch by the use of a smaller sheet of paper, smaller type, a monogram in place of the firm's standard letterhead, a handwritten envelope address, colored stationery, and a return address on the back flap of the envelope.

b. In letters to women use language that is more formal and dignified than that of other letters; avoid an intimate tone, a breezy style, colloquialisms, or slang. French words are permissible in selling clothes, cosmetics, style articles, and foods appealing to the taste.

Dear Mrs. Hudson:

Now you can enjoy serving perfect, crunchy toast at any time—for breakfast, for dinner, for tea, for late-evening snacks. It's so easy to make, and the countless ways you can serve it provide variety and zest for every meal.

How simple it is to make Toastmaster Toast! Merely put the bread in the Toastmaster and press down the lever. When the toast is done just the way you like best, up it pops, ready to serve, and the current shuts off automatically. That's all there is to making perfect toast—always crisp and golden outside, hot and tender inside. It's never hard, never dry, never scorched. And it stays hot till you're ready to serve it.

For its beauty, as well as its convenience, you will want to see the Toastmaster on your dining table. The simple, modern design and the rich chromium finish lend attractiveness to any setting. Know the inimitable flavor of Toastmaster Toast, and the matchless ease of making it.

You will find the new Toastmaster at Black and Brown in your city. Stop in and see it!

Very truly yours,

WATERS GENTER COMPANY

c. Use persuasion and emotional appeals rather than logical argument in letters to women. Such letters sell visions of the satisfaction that the product will give in utility and beauty; and they express those visions in terms of concrete things, such as leisure hours, easy housework, and freedom from worry, heat, or dust.

[92]

LETTERS TO WOMEN

Dear Mrs. Graham:

Are you good at imagining? Then picture a lustrous, silvery sink in your own kitchen. Can't you just see how it will "dress up" the most-used room in your house?

A Monel Metal Sink will make your kitchen color scheme more charming, too, for Monel Metal harmonizes with all kitchen colors—adding the silvery brightness that is just the modern note your kitchen needs.

These new standardized Monel Metal Sinks have aroused the interest of women everywhere. For the feminine eye sees in these new sinks all the features that will make housekeeping easier—features never before available in any one kitchen sink—for instance: silvery beauty; chip- and crack-proof surfaces; corrosion- and stain-resistance; freedom from rust; noise-killing insulation; no seams or sharp corners; and, of great importance, thirty-one per cent more usable surface for an equal amount of floor space.

To the thousands of women who have previously considered Monel Metal Sinks an out-of-reach luxury, it is great news that moderate prices are now made possible by standardized factory production.

Perhaps you are already acquainted with Monel Metal—the perfect household metal—through your experience with Monel Metal washing machines, table tops, cabinet tops, and other household equipment. If so, then you know it pays to look for this evidence of quality when buying new furnishings.

Ask your plumber about the new sinks and, in the meantime, be sure to mail the coupon for booklets giving more information.

Very truly yours,

THE INTERNATIONAL NICKEL
COMPANY, INC.

d. Appeal to the motives of maternal love, the desire for the beautiful, thrift, labor-saving instincts, the desire for

[92]

the welfare of the home and the family, curiosity, and the love of style and exclusiveness.

Dear Mrs. Knowlton:

Probably you, too, have discovered that it *is* possible to save money on food these days—and yet serve attractive, satisfying dishes. The secret is this: Choose foods that are favorites no matter what they cost but that are now selling at bargain prices.

Today, when California Lima Beans are so very reasonable in price, they are one of the biggest food bargains you can bring to your table. They offer an ideal solution to the problem so many home managers are facing at present—how to keep the food bills down and yet have meals every day that are as healthful and appetizing as they should be.

Just try Limas! Their economy will delight you. And no matter how you serve Limas—as a hearty main-course dish, in a delicious soup or refreshing salad—you're sure of a treat in wholesome goodness and flavor. Limas have always been famous for those qualities.

Limas, of course, save you kitchen time, as well as money. There's no bothersome preparation—no peeling, paring, or cutting. Put them to soak after breakfast, and by mid-afternoon they're ready to cook. And because Limas *are* so easy to fix, it's a good idea to cook up an extra cupful. Put these aside, and presto!—there you have the makings of a quick salad tomorrow, and enough for a savory Lima soup for luncheon or supper the day after.

From every point of view—flavor, economy, and healthfulness—Limas are an ideal food for your everyday menus. Serve them often—but always be sure, when you call your grocer, to ask for Seaside Brand.

Very truly yours,

CALIFORNIA LIMA BEAN GROWERS ASSOCIATION

e. Samples, trial use, guarantees, and testimonials from prominent women are effective forms of evidence in letters to women.

Dear Mrs. Grant:

If you are ever tempted to choose a refrigerator merely because of "low price," it will pay you to stop for a minute and ask yourself these questions:

Does it have the power that approaches Frigidaire's in all-weather efficiency and all-time operating efficiency?

Does it have a finish that can compare with the healthful cleanliness and the enduring beauty of lifetime porcelain, inside and out? Does it have an acid-resisting Porcelain-on-steel food compartment?

Does it have conveniences equal to Frigidaire's famous Cold Control . . . its Quickube Tray for easy removal of ice cubes . . . its stainless metal trays? Will it keep vegetables as fresh and crisp as the patented Frigidaire Hydrator?

In fairness to yourself, check these questions *before* you buy! Only Frigidaire answers all of them in the way you want them answered. And only Frigidaire is backed by a three-year General Motors guarantee. You'll find that, after all, the greatest bargain is Frigidaire's extra value.

Very truly yours,

FRIGIDAIRE CORPORATION

Letters to Dealers

93a. **In writing letters to dealers, appeal to the desire for profits.** Show the dealer that the product will sell readily and that the sales will be profitable. Statements made to dealers need to be supported by evidence.

[93]

Gentlemen:

Are you satisfied with your last year's profits? . . . Do you feel that you have obtained the best results possible?

If not . . . if you are interested in better results . . . read this letter carefully.

Last year, many dealers felt that their companies were loading them . . . pushing them too hard . . . expecting too much and giving too little. They felt a lack of co-operation.

Today, they are handling different lines of tires.

Goodrich improves the dealer's salesmanship by systematic sales training . . . by proved merchandising plans . . . and by effective demonstrating tools.

Goodrich helps to improve store management, repair service, and use of advertising.

Goodrich coöperates with powerful, excellently directed advertising of every nature, local and national.

Goodrich, too, offers dealers these advantages . . . the exclusive sale of Air Containers (the overwhelming sales leader in puncture-sealing tubes) . . . the famous SILVERTOWN and GOODRICH truck tires that showed remarkable gains last year . . . and are repeating that advance this year.

At the first opportunity, talk with the Goodrich salesman.

Very truly yours,

THE B. F. GOODRICH RUBBER COMPANY

b. Attract the dealer's attention to the letter by offering some help or service such as the following:

1. Advertising:
   - (a) National or sectional.
   - (b) Partial payment for local advertising.
   - (c) Copy and cuts for local advertising.

2. Form letters covering a list of the dealer's prospects.
3. Aids in window display.
4. Folders and booklets.
5. Samples.
6. Canvassers and demonstrators.
7. Offer of more customers.
8. Trial orders.
9. Referring to local dealers, answers to national magazine advertising.

Dear Mr. Roselle:

We enclose two new folders and a blotter, prepared to help sheet metal contractors tie in with Anaconda Copper advertising to the general public. Please note that they stress the service that YOU can render YOUR customers. We shall be glad to send you a supply of each, imprinted with your firm name and address, without cost.

May we also call your attention to the enclosed Anaconda Copper advertisement, which appeared in *The Saturday Evening Post?* Similar advertisements, in such nationally read publications as *Better Homes and Gardens, House and Garden, House Beautiful, The American Home,* and *Home and Field,* are carrying the story of Anaconda Copper to nearly five million homes. In all, Anaconda will publish this year approximately 39,500,000 advertising pages to home owners and prospective home owners.

Nation-wide advertising during the past ten years has created a preference for Anaconda Copper. We believe that it will be to your advantage to tie in with this advertising by using the free folders and blotters we offer. Order your supply today. For your convenience, an order card is enclosed.

Yours very truly,

THE AMERICAN BRASS COMPANY

Letters to Farmers

94a. Use reason-why copy in letters to farmers. Present carefully substantiated facts and figures.

[94]

b. Since the goods must satisfy the farmer's needs, make utility your dominant appeal. Price, quality, and service are also important considerations.

c. Use guarantees and free trials as essential means of conviction in letters to farmers. Testimonials from reputable sources are frequently effective.

d. Adapt your letter to the farmer, not only in language, but also in subject matter. However, remember that an effective letter never condescends or talks down to the farmer.

e. Make your message so clear that your letter contains no obscure phrases or ambiguous statements admitting of more than one interpretation.

f. Letters to farmers are usually much longer than letters to other classes. They may be two pages in length or even longer.

Dear Mr. Fullsher:

Getting 58 years of average service out of a McCormick-Deering BALL-BEARING separator in about 4 years is unusual—but read the letter from Anton J. Johnson, Manager, Macomb Dairy Company, Macomb, Illinois.

"Our No. 6 McCormick-Deering cream separator, purchased from you in December, 1927, is still in daily service. A conservative estimate of the amount of milk put through this separator in four years is 425,000 gallons. At 60 degrees Fahrenheit our butter fat loss is less than $\frac{1}{100}$ of 1 per cent. The remarkable thing, however, is that without special attention this separator has never been out of service a single day in four years. If this separator ever wears out (which seems doubtful) we certainly would put in another McCormick-Deering."

With an average production of 5,188 pounds of milk per cow, per year, it would take 12 cows a total of 58 years to produce 425,000 gallons of milk. In other words, Mr.

Johnson's McCormick-Deering cream separator has done in 4 years the work that would be required in 58 years on a 12-cow dairy farm. Space does not permit us to enumerate all the many desirable features of this cream separator, but the enclosed folder includes information that will be of special interest.

Farming today and in the future holds the greatest promise for the man who takes advantage of every possible means of lowering his production costs. The McCormick-Deering line of farm operating equipment offers many opportunities for reducing crop production costs. In addition, it presents possibilities for making the difficult farm tasks easier and speeding up the seasonal operations that frequently have an influence on crop yield and quality, thus bringing proportionately better returns from both equipment and labor.

There is no expense involved, except your time, in becoming posted on what is latest and best in equipment. You can do this at "Farm Machine Headquarters"—the above-named McCormick-Deering dealer's store. You and your family are always welcome. You can secure practical information and see the machines best adapted to your needs. Make it a point to come in and get better acquainted and look over the facilities available for McCormick-Deering service.

Yours very truly,

INTERNATIONAL HARVESTER COMPANY

Letters to Businessmen

95a. In selling to a business man an article not to be resold but one to be used in the conduct of his own business, the most effective appeals are utility and efficiency.

b. Present forceful evidence that the article will fill the reader's needs. Facts, figures, and testimonials from prominent users are effective.

Gentlemen:

More than 2,000,000 Everdur bolts have been placed in

[95]

transmission line service during the past three years. To date, not a single one of the bolts has been reported as failing.

The properties of Everdur Metal, which make such a record possible, are concisely described in the enclosed new booklet "Everdur Bolts, Screws, and Accessories." If you have outdoor engineering problems, we believe that you will find the information contained in the booklet well worth your serious consideration.

Everdur Metal is moderate in cost and economical to fabricate. Because of its high strength, resistance to corrosion, and immunity to seasonal cracking, Everdur was adopted by a switching equipment manufacturer to supplant a cheaper alloy used for the bolts in certain types of switches. Fabrication economies possible with Everdur not only absorbed the difference in the cost between the two metals, but, in addition, provided an average saving in the cost of the finished bolts of 14.75% for 1,000 pieces.

If you are interested in applications of Everdur other than those mentioned in the enclosed booklet, we shall be glad to forward you further literature, or write you fully regarding any specific application you may mention.

Yours very truly,

THE AMERICAN BRASS COMPANY

c. Make letters to business men brief. The main work of selling is left to enclosures. Express your ideas directly and concisely.

Dear Mr. Ward:

As a business man who is vitally interested in saving money for his organization, you'll find a very interesting story in the enclosed folder.

It presents a method that cuts the cost of billing to a minimum—often right in half.

After you have read the folder, may we show more definitely how Multi-PLY will apply to your business—without upsetting your present methods or adding one bit of red tape?

Just okay and return this letter. A practical suggestion here and there by our systems staff may save your organization hundreds of dollars every year.

Very truly yours,

THE GLOBE REGISTER COMPANY

Letters to Professional People

96a. Letters to lawyers, doctors, dentists, ministers, teachers, artists, actors, architects, and musicians appeal to efficiency, economy, orderliness, and beauty. The emotional appeal may be used if judiciously combined with substantiated facts. Phrase the letters in a manner that seems to allow full independence of decision.

Dear Mr. Eubank:

You will be interested in the announcement that Mr. Dugald A. Shaw has joined our organization as Chief Engineer.

For the past twelve years Mr. Shaw has held a similar position with the Weary & Alford Company, Architects, specializing in the design and equipment of banks, public buildings, and similar structures in which metal work and equipment are a distinctive feature.

Changing styles in architecture have brought about the use of new metals. The character of buildings now being erected—hospitals, post offices, court houses, libraries, and commercial office buildings—brings you new problems in the layout, design, and construction of metal work that Art Metal knows how to meet.

We welcome an opportunity to be of service through our well-balanced Engineering Department, of which Mr. Shaw is now the head. In addition, we offer the findings of continuous research and the facilities of the largest and best equipped factory of its kind in the country.

One of our twenty-four branch offices is near you and will respond promptly if we can be of immediate service on any project. May we hear from you?

Yours very truly,

ART METAL CONSTRUCTION COMPANY

b. Use a professional appeal in letters such as those that are to sell office supplies to doctors and dentists or reference books to lawyers and teachers.

Dear Doctor Nile:

"Doctor, what shall I do for my cold?" At this season of the year your patients ask you that troublesome question many times.

The local symptoms of colds in the head are quickly relieved by the use of EfeDroN Hart Nasal Jelly. EfeDroN promptly relieves the nasal congestion by contracting capillaries, reducing turbinates, and diminishing hyperemia. It quickly opens the nasal air passages and establishes sufficient ventilation and drainage to make normal breathing effortless.

The water-soluble demulcent jelly base gives free and maximal Ephedrine action, allays irritation, and avoids the insulating effect of oily bases on the active ingredient, Ephedrine Hydrochloride. The Ephedrine action is prolonged with a minimum of reaction.

Try EfeDroN as a local aid in conjunction with your systemic treatment for patients suffering with colds, sinusitis, or naso-pharyngitis.

Mail the enclosed card for a free tube. Your druggist is prepared to fill your prescriptions.

Very truly yours,[1]

[1] From *Postage and the Mailbag.*

c. **The letter may also appeal to the professional man's personal needs and interests. In such a letter, the appeal is the same as that of letters directed to educated people in general.**

d. **Confine the letter to a page in length; place most of the evidence in enclosures. All fill-ins must be perfectly matched, so that the letter appears to be an individual letter.**

Letters to Executives

97. **Letters to executives and bankers must be concerned with the product's worth, appropriateness, reliability, and fairness of price. Keep the language dignified and the attitude one of respectful restraint. The letters should be less than a page in length, enclosures being used for the detailed work of evidence. The stationery should be of high quality. Remember, also, that people of this class are accustomed to making their own decisions.**

Dear Mr. Reilly:

No matter how carefully a heating system is planned, it seems inevitable that some parts of a building will receive too much heat while other parts are receiving hardly enough.

The overheating of any part of a building is not only costly in the matter of wasted fuel, but it is unhealthful and causes drowsiness. It can be prevented by Minneapolis-Honeywell sectional automatic control of valves supplying heat to various zones within the building, or by automatic control of the individual radiators that tend to overheat, or by a combination of both.

Different parts of a building may require different temperatures to be maintained within them. A study by Minneapolis-Honeywell temperature control engineers of the desired conditions for operating in your new building will reveal the nature of the controls you need to attain the efficient, economical, healthful heating you want in all parts of the building at all times.

A survey of your plans by the Minneapolis-Honeywell representative will cost you nothing, and will assure you of heating satisfaction.

Yours very truly,

MINNEAPOLIS-HONEYWELL
REGULATOR CO.

Letters to Salesmen

98a. Letters to salesmen should view their problems with understanding and consideration. The attitude should be human, diplomatic, and coöperative. The message should be helpful—analyzing or solving some problem or need. There should be present an element of inspiration that will appeal to the reader's imagination. Often, suggestion is more effective than direct statement.

Dear Mr. Black:

You have recently decided to represent this company in Idaho. We are mighty glad to have you with us and hope that you will never regret your decision.

In order that you may know more about our facilities, we are attaching to this letter a multigraphed sheet itemizing all the services we offer to Standard agents in the way of creative advertising and a unique insurance marketing. We have already sent you a packet of samples consisting of blotters, circulars, folders, booklets—in fact, an assortment that will give you a visual picture of campaign material.

Our whole advertising force is made up of people who have come from the advertising field into this insurance business. They know the "ins" and "outs" of printed selling—how it can be most effectively applied to local businesses. They are considered experts in their work.

With such an experienced force directing it, Standard has put the enormous sum of a quarter million dollars into advertising in the past two years.

Our services are effective and unique—worth every penny we have put into them and every cent the agents are spending on them.

We want you to feel free to call upon us at any time for any one of the services listed on the attached sheet or for any advertising you have in mind that we have not mentioned.

Very truly yours,

STANDARD ACCIDENT
INSURANCE CO.

b. According to the particular situation, the letters may vary in length from brief "pep" talks to detailed explanations of selling plans in their relation to prices, territory to be covered, and proper methods to be used in selling difficult customers.

c. When necessary, write letters to salesmen that will encourage greater efforts, express appreciation, increase their confidence in the goods they sell, suggest improvement, or discipline them. Letters may also be written to give information about goods, customers, competitors, and the selling operations of the house.

Letters to Composite Classes

99. Frequently the letter is addressed to a class of readers not distinguishable by sex or occupation. To write such a letter, study the particular type of prospects to whom the letter is addressed and decide whether the tone is to be sedate, conservative, progressive, colloquial, sprightly, breezy, or buoyant.

[99]

Dear Mr. Folsom:

It's your bread line—

It will be only a few days now until men begin coming to us begging for just one square meal. Hungry men. Jobless men. That's the kind we help—almost the only kind we know, at Union Gospel Mission.

Have you ever stood in a bread line?

Have you ever faced a norther without an overcoat? If you have, you will not need a second call.

You will thank us for handling this winter's bread line for you. For it is your bread line, after all. You will thank us for turning desperate men from a road that leads toward a prison cot to a fresh start and self-support when a job opens.

For hungry men are simply jail fodder.

Now, how much would you give to see the light of hope once more in five pairs of eyes? It can be done through the plain and homely service of filling five hungry stomachs with hot, wholesome food. And for how much?

One dollar is all I am asking of you.

But that one dollar will be needed—badly needed, very soon. That one dollar multiplied by one thousand who know what it is to be down and out—one thousand who want to help somebody a little less lucky—that means five thousand meals.

Of all years, this year the bread line will be the most urgent. No need to emphasize that. Of all years, this year your dollar will do the most.

Just one dollar. Will you?

Sincerely yours,[2]

[2] From *Postage and the Mailbag.*

Sales Series

The Wear-out Sales Series

100a. Each letter of the wear-out series is a complete sales letter.

Dear Mr. White:

When you were a youngster and were laid up because of an accident, your only worry was how soon you'd have to go back to school. And later on, in high school and college, when you cracked a couple of ribs in a football skirmish, you fretted because you'd miss the next game with the fellows.

No worries then about the bills or your job. Dad took care of the expenses, and school was always there to go back to.

Now, it's different. You are earning a living and you have responsibilities that you cannot evade. If you have an accident, you must somehow pay the doctor, the nurse, and the hospital. On top of that, the living expenses for you and your family go on. How you will meet them is one of the things you must face while you still have the opportunity to prepare for such emergencies.

You will be interested in our new insurance coverage called the "Safeguard Policy" because it safeguards your earnings against the costs of personal accidents.

The Safeguard Policy will pay all your expenses as long as you are laid up, regardless of whether or not your earnings continue. If your injury is caused by an automobile or public conveyance, you receive double the weekly sum.

[100]

It's easy to procrastinate—but not very wise. Send the card now for complete facts about this new policy for the modern man—before you forget!

Very truly yours,

STANDARD ACCIDENT INSURANCE CO.

b. Each letter uses a different appeal or selling point. Sometimes a strong selling point is reworded and presented from a new viewpoint.

Dear Mr. Brown:

For the first time, during the next thirty days, we offer you a complete accountancy lesson service—free.

This offer is made to a selected few who have inquired about our accountancy training and have not enrolled. Under this special offer, you have the opportunity to determine to your own satisfaction and without cost or obligation your own fitness and aptitude for the highly paid positions in accountancy.

If you wish, you may work out the questions and problems and send in your solutions for grading and personal criticism by a C.P.A.—free of cost—just as if you were already a regularly enrolled LaSalle member.

There are no strings on this offer—no catch of any kind in it. We just want you to see for yourself what our training is like and how you fit into that training. We hope you will be so pleased that you will enroll—but that's up to you.

All you need do is sign and mail the enclosed card. The complete lesson will be forwarded immediately. This is your chance to test yourself.

Yours very truly,

LASALLE EXTENSION UNIVERSITY

[100]

THE WEAR-OUT SALES SERIES

Dear Mr. Brown:

If you could take a trip through LaSalle and see our equipment and resources, meet our instructors and personnel, you would surely enroll at once for Higher Accountancy.

Since you can't make this trip, the next best thing is to read the enclosed booklet, "My Trip Through LaSalle." Lots of pictures and a few words show you how we work and play. See all the departments and the experts who are so interested in you and your success, and who will go to any lengths to give you the personal, careful, human help you need. When you reach the last page, you'll feel personally acquainted with us all.

Some literature is being mailed to you separately. It tells just what you want to know about the field that interests you, the opportunities in it for you, and how our training plan fits you for those opportunities with the famous LaSalle Problem Method. This method is the latest development in business training. From the fine financial gains and mental growth it has brought thousands of others, we know it will "work" for you, too.

Read the literature and see how this plan will use the education and experience you already have to best advantage and enable you to carry out your future plans.

Then tell me about your decision. If you want any more information about the training, or about how it will benefit you, tell me that too. Your letter will bring the best of my long experience in my immediate and personal reply.

Very truly yours,

LASALLE EXTENSION UNIVERSITY

c. The wear-out series is used mainly to sell medium-priced and low-priced articles appealing to a diversified list.

d. **The letters are sent to the same list of prospects until the returns are no longer profitable and the list is thus worn out.**

e. **The length of the series is usually not planned in advance.**

The Continuous Sales Series

101a. Each letter of the continuous sales series is a complete and independent sales letter.

Letter No. 1

Dear Mr. Murtagh:

"FROM MINE TO YOUR HOME" is the title of a new booklet now in preparation, which will be sent to you in a few days.

You will find this booklet extremely interesting. Fully illustrated, it tells you the story of coal from the time it was discovered up to the present time. It takes you to the anthracite mines of Pennsylvania, shows you how the coal is mined, how it is cleaned of impurities, sorted into sizes, shipped to us—finally delivered to your home.

Divided into nine chapters, it is easy to read. Educational, every member of your family will enjoy it. Attractively bound, it will make a worthy addition to your library.

May we remind you that now is an excellent time to order whatever coal you will need during the remainder of the winter? You will find HOT-TEST Anthracite truly fine coal, full of heat, and most economical to burn.

An order card is enclosed. Why not fill in the number of tons you will want during the remainder of the year and return it to us? Our telephone is Mott Haven 679. We'll deliver it promptly.

Very truly yours,

THE CONTINUOUS SALES SERIES

Letter No. 2

Dear Mr. Murtagh:

You are about ready now to forget your coal bin until another season.

That's fine. But here's a little detail you should attend to first.

ORDER YOUR COAL SUPPLY FOR NEXT WINTER AND SAVE MONEY BY TAKING ADVANTAGE OF THE NEW LOW SPRING PRICES, WHICH GO INTO EFFECT APRIL 1.

Enclosed is a return card. Jot down on it your requirements and return it to us, and we shall deliver your coal any time before June 1 at the present low prices. The new low prices are listed on the card.

These prices will be advanced June 5. It will pay you well in money saved to place your order now. In addition, the quality of coal for summer delivery is of the finest—absolutely clean and full of heat.

Drop the card into the mail today and we will do the rest. Not even a stamp is needed in returning it to us.

Very truly yours,

Letter No. 3

Dear Mr. Murtagh:

About three weeks ago we mailed you a reply card that has not yet been returned to us.

Many of our customers have already sent their orders for early delivery. An early delivery is YOUR best assurance of lowest prices and full supply.

If you have just forgotten to mail the card, do it at once. If you feel uncertain of your place of residence another season, or wish to make some changes in the kinds or sizes of coal you will use next winter, just jot it down on the card enclosed and send it along. Delivery on your order will be made to suit your convenience as nearly as possible.

Now is an excellent time to have your furnace checked to see if the pipes are clogged or if the furnace is sooty. One of our experienced heating engineers will gladly make an inspection of your heating system without charge. If a vacuum cleaning is necessary, he will quote a nominal charge for this service.

You will save money, secure better heat, and eliminate all coal worries by making plans now for your next winter's heating problems.

Don't forget the card!

Very truly yours,

Letter No. 4

Dear Mr. Murtagh:

If you have not ordered your coal for next winter—you can save money by placing your order now. You can secure the finest quality anthracite, good clean coal, full of heat—better coal than we can probably get from the mines later on.

And with your bins filled, you can sit back "all set" for Old Man Winter when he arrives. You won't have a worry about next year's supply of coal.

There is still time for you to take advantage of the price reduction.

We wish also to express our deep appreciation for the business you have given us. And may we at the same time express the hope that we may care for your future requirements? For our part, we will do everything we can to merit your patronage.

We hope you will instruct us to enter your order. Our telephone number is Mott Haven 679.

Very truly yours,[1]

[1] From *Postage and the Mailbag.*

b. Letters are sent continuously to the same list of customers month by month, season by season, or year by year. Letters of this type are appropriate for the seasons of the year, holidays, graduations, marriages, birthdays, and special occasions. They are used to inform the customer of prices, special sales, and new lines of goods.

Dear Mr. Peterson:

Is there a new baby in your family?

If so, you as a parent will be interested in knowing of the new insurance plans recently announced by The Penn Mutual for children, which may be started the day a child is born.

These new plans fall into the category of Thrift-Saving-Plans, and they can be ideally adapted to guarantee a College Educational Fund when the little one reaches eighteen.

The plans also provide funds to be available when children really need money . . . to set up in business . . . to purchase a home . . . for a wedding gift . . . or any other worthwhile causes in which you are interested.

In most cases, you can have a Child Protective Agreement Clause added, which will guarantee that in the event you are making the deposits toward such a plan and do not live, we will continue the deposits and mature the contract according to your wishes.

May we send you literature descriptive of Penn Mutual Junior Insurance Plans and also our free booklet, "Child Health and Care," a summary of essential information about babies and children up to age five? Just mail the card, and the literature will reach you promptly.

Very truly yours,

THE PENN MUTUAL LIFE
INSURANCE COMPANY

c. **The letters are changed with each mailing throughout the year, and each letter has its own purpose.**

d. **The continuous series is employed to build good will, to keep accounts active, to make seasonable or timely offerings, and to keep the name of the house before its customers.**

e. **The continuous series is adapted to selling articles for which the demand is recurring or constant.**

f. **The letters should never be treated as matter-of-fact announcements.**

The Sales Campaign Series

102a. **The campaign series is designed to accomplish *as a whole* the four functions of selling. It is completely planned in advance to work as a unit toward a definite end.**

b. **The single letters of the series are not in themselves complete sales letters.** Each successive letter makes only one point or performs only one function of selling, but there is a definite connection between the letters of the series, each letter paving the way for the next.

c. **The letters of the series progress to a climax from the first letter securing attention and interest, through the letters arousing desire and establishing conviction, to the final letter stimulating action.**

d. **The number of letters in the series is determined by the object of the campaign (for example, pioneering work or competitive sales), the nature of the product, the price of the article, the margin of profit, the cost of each mailing piece, and the type of prospects (market).**

e. The campaign series is used to sell high-priced products and services and to do educational or pioneering work. Enclosures are often employed with letters of this series.

Letter No. 1 (ATTENTION)

Dear Mr. Lockwood:

You CAN have warm rooms to dress in.

If there were nothing else you could do about it, you might become reconciled to the hardship of depriving yourself of another hour of needed and deserved sleep every morning to run, shivering, downstairs to open the draft of your furnace. For somebody (or something) must certainly open the draft every morning.

But fortunately there is something else you can do about it!

A Minneapolis-Honeywell Temperature Regulator will AUTOMATICALLY, at bedtime, close down the draft of your furnace to give you just the fuel-saving temperature you want. Early in the morning (while you still sleep) it will AUTOMATICALLY open the draft, bringing the temperature up to just the comfortable degree you desire—no higher.

Then automatically, throughout the day, it will STEADILY hold the temperature at the healthful, comfortable degree you want it, preventing overheating as well as underheating.

Very truly yours,

MINNEAPOLIS-HONEYWELL
REGULATOR CO.

Letter No. 2 (DESIRE)

Dear Mr. Lockwood:

Free your wife from the continual nuisance and drudgery of trying to regulate the home temperature by hand.

Let her go out all day knowing that during her absence the heating plant will be AUTOMATICALLY and safely regulated, keeping the house steadily at just the temperature you desire.

The Minneapolis-Honeywell Heat Regulator will do these things for her without attention.

You needn't get up early in a cold house to start the fire. The Regulator will do it for you, automatically, while you still sleep. After dressing and breakfasting comfortably in a warm house, put some coal on the fire—less coal than you now do, for the Regulator, by preventing overheating, saves considerable fuel—and then you can forget your heating plant all day.

Very truly yours,

MINNEAPOLIS-HONEYWELL
REGULATOR CO.

Letter No. 3 (CONVICTION)

Dear Mr. Lockwood:

Here's why—

A Minneapolis-Honeywell Temperature Regulator usually saves 20% or more in fuel cost.

Without clock control of your furnace, when you get up in your cold house, you hurriedly shake down the fire, losing some live coals through the grates in your haste. You throw on fresh coals, and perhaps, to get extreme draft, you open the ash-pit door. Surplus heat goes up the flue, and unburned coal goes out as ashes.

Minneapolis-Honeywell clock control warms your house before you arise, with the coal you put on the night before. When you tend the furnace in the morning, it is only to bank the fire for the day.

Without automatic regulation, about the middle of the morning some member of your household who does not operate in the way you do, starts monkeying with it, likely throwing on too much coal.

The Minneapolis-Honeywell will automatically, steadily, maintain the proper temperature throughout the day, with no attention.

While you are asleep, without automatic control it is impossible to adjust the drafts in accordance with changes in weather. If the weather turns warmer than you expected during the night, you are wasting fuel.

But the Minneapolis-Honeywell will close down the drafts promptly if the weather turns warm, thus saving fuel.

And your fire will not burn itself out so often and require rebuilding when it is automatically controlled.

The Minneapolis-Honeywell will save money for you, as well as provide convenience, comfort, and safety.

Very truly yours,

MINNEAPOLIS-HONEYWELL
REGULATOR CO.

Letter No. 4 (ACTION)

Dear Mr. Lockwood:

Leaders of the medical profession unanimously condemn the too common practice of overheating homes. They know that living in overheated rooms causes colds by destroying one's natural mucous defense against them. They have also proved that overheating saps energy and causes "that tired feeling."

There is only one sure way to prevent overheating your home, and that is by AUTOMATIC control of the heating plant. No matter how hard you try, by hand operation of check and draft dampers, the fire will frequently "get away from you" and heat your rooms up unhealthfully.

The Minneapolis-Honeywell Heat Regulator will automatically, continually, steadily maintain just the healthful, moderate, economical, and safe degree of temperature you desire. You NEVER need touch the dampers!

In the light of present medical knowledge, a hand-regulated heating plant is a serious menace to the health of your family.

The convenience, comfort, safety, health, and fuel economy that are provided by automatic temperature control will all be gladly explained to you by the Minneapolis-Honeywell man. You'll find his name in the telephone book. Call him today.

Very truly yours,

MINNEAPOLIS-HONEYWELL
REGULATOR CO.

The Time Interval

103a. Wear-out letters are sent at brief intervals, one week or less apart.

b. Continuous letters are sent at irregular intervals.

c. The time interval between letters of the sales campaign series depends upon:

(1) **The kind of product.** If the product is of such a kind that a decision can be made quickly, the interval may be just long enough for the reader to reply.

(2) **The type of prospect.** For example, letters to farmers allow a longer interval to elapse than do letters to business men.

(3) **The selling method.** If the appeal is suggestive and emotional, the interval is brief. When argument and the reason-why appeal are used, the interval is longer, because the reader must be convinced and have time to arrive at a decision.

(4) **Seasonal demand.** Letters must be sent before the beginning of the seasonal buying period and usually at brief intervals.

(5) **The distance of the reader from the firm.** Sufficient time for the reader to reply should elapse between successive letters.

The Mailing List

104a. The mailing list must be composed of real prospects.

b. The mailing list must be built upon certain characteristics common to the prospects, thus enabling the writer to choose the most effective selling appeals. The prospects must have a need or a desire for the product or be susceptible of being educated to a need or a desire; their incomes must be sufficient to enable them to purchase the product; they must be analyzed and classified, as the product suggests, on common economic, financial, educational, professional, commercial, or social levels; they must constitute a market as determined by these common characteristics.

c. The names and addresses of the list must be complete, correct, and up to date. All names and addresses should be checked and verified.

d. The mailing list may be purchased from professional mailing list companies (mailing list compilers sell lists for almost every line of trade).

e. The mailing list may be compiled by the seller himself. Following are the principal sources of names for the mailing list:

The firm's own records of its customers

Records of credit customers
Records of cash customers
C.O.D. slips and delivery reports
Salesmen's reports
Contest returns
Canvassers' records
Inquiries and answers to advertising
Names obtained from present customers

Directories

City
Telephone
Trade
Mercantile
Professional
Institutional
Club
Social
University and college

Membership rolls

Clubs, societies, lodges, and fraternal organizations
Church organizations
Payrolls of firms
Chambers of commerce and service clubs
Labor unions

Governmental records and lists

Licenses and permits
Vital statistics
Tax lists
Voters' lists
City and county employees
School lists
Building permits
Mortgages
Bankruptcies
Incorporations
Real estate transfers

General

Advertising
Newspapers
Trade journals
Canvassers and contests
Rating books
Dealers
Exchange with other firms

Tests

105a. Test the letters of the series on a small list, selecting average prospects and average localities. Ten per cent of the entire list is usually a fair test.

b. Carefully record and analyze the returns from each letter. For this purpose, key the letters or use return post cards, addressed envelopes, envelopes of different colors, and similar enclosures. Have the replies addressed to a certain department or a certain person in the firm.

c. **If the list is representative, the percentage of returns from the test should indicate what to expect from the large list.**

d. **Rewrite the letters that were weak or unsuccessful.**

e. **Be sure that similar conditions prevail for the test and for the complete mailing, that business conditions are the same, that the geographical distribution of the letters is similar, and that the readers receive the letters at similar times.**

"Splits"

106. **When the series "splits," that is, produces an unexpected inquiry asking for special information, drop the original series and give the inquirer individual attention by means of a personally dictated letter, a form letter, or a new series covering the subject of his unexpected inquiry.**

Linking the Letters

107a. **When the letter opening refers to a preceding letter, the link material should grasp the attention and the interest of the reader.**

> If you have been interested in this short discussion of fire insurance, we ask that you give our representative, Mr. Wiltsie, an opportunity to tell you some more about our insurance.
>
> Let us now get to a very vital point—how much money we can save you.
>
> Some time ago we made the statement that you could make a friend out of a man by asking him to do you a favor.
>
> Here's why—
>
> A Minneapolis-Honeywell temperature regulator usually saves 20% or more in fuel cost.

b. **Certain negative and tactless openings are to be avoided:**

(1) Irritation at not receiving a reply.

It is more than ten days since we honestly pleaded with you to consider your own welfare and the welfare of those whom you might injure, as well as that of your family, by buying insurance protection.

(2) Attempt to put the reader under obligation.

If we do not receive the card enclosed with this letter, we shall assume that we have your assent in sending the set of reference books.

(3) Suggestion that the letter went astray.

We cannot help feeling, Mr. Burns, that you have mislaid this letter or have not seen it at all, or else you would have acknowledged it.

(4) Implication that failure to reply was due to discourtesy.

The booklets were mailed two weeks ago, and we have been expecting your acceptance before this. You could at least give us the courtesy of a reply.

(5) Implication that failure to reply was due to stupidity.

We cannot imagine anyone who is mentally alive failing to reply or to take advantage of this offer.

(6) Suggestion that the letters are annoying.

I do hate to keep harping on one subject, Mr. Durst, but I can't help writing to you once more.

Application Letters

Analyzing the Problem

108a. Get all possible information about the employer. Analyze his character, personality, and temperament so that you can adapt your letter to him. Become familiar with the firm's policies, organization, and methods.

b. Analyze thoroughly the requirements of the position. Read the advertisement with care; seek information from your friends and acquaintances and from employees.

c. If you are not applying for a known vacancy in a particular firm but are working the field of potential employers in order to uncover a lead, prepare a mailing list of prospective employers and an application letter adapted to the nature of the position you desire to secure and to the general character of the firms on the mailing list. The letters may be sent to the entire list in one mailing, or they may be mailed to selected portions of the list at intervals. Sometimes it is desirable to test the letter on a representative portion of the list in order to determine its drawing power; if the returns indicate that the letter is ineffective or faulty, it should be rewritten or revised.

d. Analyze your selling points. From your general qualifications—age, education, training, experience, character, personality—and special qualifications, select those particular points that focus directly upon the position for which you are applying.

e. **Present these qualifications in the light of their service to the employer and of their ability to satisfy the requirements of the position. Make these selling points persuade the employer that you are the man he wants.**

f. **Make a list of good references.**

The Physical Make-up

109a. **The stationery should be a plain white sheet of good quality and of standard size, 8½ by 11 inches. Type the letter neatly and arrange the material in one of the standard forms.**

b. **Always use the full heading (street address; city, postal delivery zone number, and state; and the date).**

1445 Morrison Avenue
Chicago 12, Illinois
May 14, 19—

c. **It is wise to use both a handwritten and a typed signature.**

Very truly yours,

Paul T. Bates

Paul T. Bates

d. **Correctness in spelling, grammar, punctuation, and all other details is important.**

e. **Do not use fraternity, hotel, or personal stationery, or the stationery of some firm.**

Principles of Applications

110a. **The application letter is a sales letter. It sells to the prospective employer the applicant's ability, knowledge, experience, training, skill, and personality.**

b. **The application letter must have the *you* attitude and must be positive in tone. The *you* attitude does not mean the avoidance of the pronoun *I*; it means, rather, the presentation of the applicant's qualifications in the light of their service to the prospective employer.**

c. **Do not make the application letter general. It is always more effective to apply for a specific position than to make a general offer of one's services. The applicant's qualifications must be so selected and presented as to focus pertinently upon the particular position for which he is applying.**

d. **State your education specifically—the names of the schools you attended, the dates of entering and leaving, your degrees, your major field, your specialized subjects, and your honors and distinctions.**

e. **State your business experience specifically. Give the name of the firm (or firms) for which you worked, the name of your immediate superior and his official title or position, the particular kind of work you did, and the definite length of time you were employed by the firm.**

f. **If you are employed, explain why you wish to leave your present position.**

g. **Leave the question of salary until the interview, unless the advertisement or the application questionnaire directs you to state the salary you desire. Never write, "Salary is no object."**

h. If the hiring is done by a specific individual or department of the firm, address the application letter to the proper person or department. Most large firms, however, process application letters through the personnel department.

i. The close of the application letter asks for an interview. If an interview, however, is impracticable, because of geographical distances or some similar reason, the letter asks for the position.

j. To make action easy, give the prospective employer your telephone number and the time and place at which you may be reached.

k. Solicited application letters are written in answer to advertisements (or other requests). The letter must carefully cover the points outlined as qualifications in the advertisement. The opening may apply for the position, and it may use a reference to the advertisement as the point of contact, but it must not be stereotyped, offensively breezy, or smug.

l. Unsolicited letters are written by the applicant on his own initiative and not in answer to advertisements or requests. The opening must be original, interesting, and indicative of the personality and ability of the applicant.

m. The blind advertisement is answered in the same way as the signed advertisement, except that adaptation to the character of the house is impossible. The salutation is "Gentlemen" or whatever other salutation is indicated by the contents of the advertisement. If you wish not to divulge your name, you may answer by a blind reply; it is advisable, however, to give a plausible reason for withholding your name.

n. In applying for a position based upon vacancy information supplied by a third person, use the informant's

name as the point of contact if it carries prestige and is favorably regarded by the prospective employer. Be sure to use the informant's correct initials, name, and title or official position.

References and Recommendations

111a. Select references who know you well enough to speak with authority.

b. References may be given for character, education, and experience.

c. Always secure permission from the reference to use his name.

d. Give the reference's name and title and his address or the address of the firm for which he works. The telephone number of the reference is often included.

e. Open letters of recommendation have little value. It is not advisable to employ "to whom it may concern" recommendations. Letters of recommendation are confidential and are mailed by the reference directly to the prospective employer.

Structure: Sales-letter Form

112. The application letter may employ a structure similar to that of the sales letter:

Attention and interest: The purpose of the beginning is to attract favorable attention and arouse interest. The beginning may definitely make application for the position. It should be direct, original, and interesting. Participial openings are weak.

Desire: Desire is created by a specific description of the applicant's qualifications—

age, education, experience, and personal characteristics. Arrange these details in a logical order and emphasize the important features.

Conviction: The prospective employer is convinced by logical reasons, evidence, or proof. Give your references here.

Action: The close of the letter asks for an interview (if an interview is impracticable, it asks for the job). To make it easy for the employer to reach you, give your telephone number, the time and place at which you may be reached, or any other pertinent information. Avoid participial and stereotyped closes.

Gentlemen:

Your advertisement in this afternoon's *Journal* is of particular interest to me. It represents an opportunity to get back into my chosen line of endeavor after spending some time in uniform.

My experience with structural steel began the summer after my graduation from high school. During that period, I worked for the MacDonald Engineering Company on a two-span steel bridge in Gabbs Valley, Nevada. Structural steel interested me very much, and at the termination of this job I attended the University of Nevada for one year, where I took a course in structural engineering. Throughout the following summer, I was employed as a bridge worker for the Kaiser Company in the San Francisco Bay area.

When this job was finished, I enlisted in the army, and after a short period of foreign service received an appointment to the United States Military Academy at West Point. This enabled me to continue my engineering education at one of the best schools in the field. After completing nearly two years of study, I was committed to the Army General Hospital with gastro-intestinal disturbances. Two months later, I was in perfect health, but judged unfit for further military duty. This resulted in a medical discharge from the service.

At the present time I am taking a refresher course at the University of California under the G.I. Bill of Rights. I am very anxious, however, to further my knowledge of structural steel in a practical manner.

The following people may be contacted concerning my qualifications:

Senator Pat McCarran
628 Hillside Drive
Reno, Nevada

Mr. Carl G. Marazza, Chief Engineer
MacDonald Engineering Co.
Gardnersville, California

General S. J. Roe, Superintendent
United States Military Academy
West Point, New York

Dr. H. B. Gibbs
Dean of the College of Engineering
University of California
Berkeley, California

I should appreciate an opportunity to see you personally so that you may receive a better idea of my ability in the field of structural engineering. You will be able to contact me at the Multnomah Hotel from December 18 until January 3.

Very truly yours,

Structure: Tabulated Form

113. The application letter may present its material in tabulated form.

Gentlemen:

The position of stenographer requires exactness and de-

[113]

pendability. Naturally, you want to obtain the most fully qualified person for the position you advertised in yesterday's *Register*. I believe I have the qualifications that will serve you best.

Age: Twenty.

Education: High school graduate, 1945, Newton High School, Newton, Kansas. One year of business college, Wichita Business College, Wichita, Kansas, July, 1945, to July, 1946. One and one-third years of college, University of Iowa, September, 1946, to December, 1947.

Experience: General clerking, Kimball's Ready-to-Wear, Newton, Kansas, Christmas rush season, December, 1944. Auditing and special reporting, Federal Public Housing, Hilltop Manor, Wichita, Kansas, temporary Civil Service appointment, July 15, 1946, to September 15, 1946. Stenographer, Midwestern Constructors, mobile office, June 17, 1947, to September 21, 1947.

References: Mrs. T. O. Ford, Head Accountant, Hilltop Manor, 3235 Wyatt Avenue, Wichita, Kansas.

Mr. J. L. Napier, Editor, *Evening Kansan Call*, Newton, Kansas.

Mr. H. J. Crum, Wichita Business College, 114 North Market Street, Wichita, Kansas.

Special qualifications: Better than average speed and accuracy in shorthand and typing. Practical knowledge of rapid calculation, accounting, and business mathematics. Ability to use comptometer, adding machine, and posting machine.

Of course, the most satisfactory way for you to determine my ability to fill a position in your firm is by a personal interview. I shall be glad to come to Des Moines whenever it is convenient for you.

Very truly yours,

Structure: Letter and Data Sheet

114a. The most effective type of application letter is the two-part letter consisting of a sales letter and an attached data sheet.

b. The data sheet contains the factual and routine, though necessary, details of the applicant's qualifications, such as personal details (name, address, telephone number, height, weight, age, birthplace, nationality, nationality of parents, marital status, and physical condition), education (schools attended, dates, degrees, major field, specialized courses, pertinent skills, honors, and distinctions), special or unusual qualifications, experience (employer, address, type of work, dates), and references (character, education, experience). The data sheet is headed *Personal Data* or *Personal Abstract*; the customary heading for the second page of a business letter is omitted. The data sheet is flexible in form, the headings and the information varying with the applicant and the position applied for.

c. The sales letter, thus freed of the burden of routine detail, concentrates upon a few strong selling points. It is a closely adapted, personalized, original selling letter, which reveals the attractive qualities of the applicant's personality, his alertness, his ambition, his initiative, his capacity, and his competence. Although the pattern is variable, the opening must attract favorable attention and the close must stimulate action.

Dear Mr. Sloan:

For eighteen months, while my father was engaged with an engineering firm prospecting for oil, I was a resident of Mexico. We traveled extensively through the country, living with Mexican families, observing their customs, and absorbing their culture.

[114]

Our contacts with all classes of people, with business, industry, and government gave us a sympathetic understanding of the Mexican people. We acquired many business and personal friends and an ability to converse fluently in Spanish.

When my family returned to the United States, I entered college with a determination to pursue a course of studies that would train me for a career in foreign trade. I took advanced work in Spanish and a major in Business Administration, with emphasis on foreign relations and foreign-trade techniques. During the past summer's vacation, while my father was in Mexico as a representative of the State Department in connection with Mexican-American trade agreements, I served as his personal secretary.

Your firm has recently announced its intention to open a branch office in Mexico City. If the information in this letter and on the attached sheet indicates my ability to fill a position in your sales organization in Mexico, I would appreciate a personal interview.

Very truly yours,

Nancy Allan

Nancy Allan

PERSONAL DATA

Personal

Name: Nancy Allan
Permanent address: Box 357, Route 3, Hood River, Oregon
Temporary address: 4385 Wisteria Drive, Portland 5, Oregon
Telephone: ALderwood 5-1337
Age: Twenty-three
Height: Five feet, five inches. Weight: 120 pounds
Nationality: American
Marital status: Single with no dependents
Physical condition: Good with no defects

Education

University of Oregon, 1947-1951
Bachelor of Arts Degree, 1951
Major field: Business Administration
Minor field: Romance languages
Specialized courses:

Personnel Management	History of South America
Traffic Management	Problems in Distribution
Foreign-trade Technique	Constructive Accounting
American Foreign Relations	Spanish (three years)
Foreign-trade Marketing	Portuguese (two years)
International Law	International Trade
Office Management	Economics

Practical Training and Experience

Personal secretary to Mr. J. P. Morton, President, First National Bank, Hood River, Oregon, June to September, 1948

Personal secretary to Mr. William T. Allan, member of Joint Mexican-American Commission on Trade Agreements, July to September, 1950

Director, Hood River Campfire Girls' Camp, July, 1949

Secretary to Mr. Thomas L. Kirby, Apple Growers' Association, Hood River, Oregon, June to September, 1950

References

Mr. J. P. Morton, President, First National Bank, 321 First Street, Hood River, Oregon

Dr. Victor P. Morris, Dean of the School of Business Administration, University of Oregon, Eugene, Oregon

Mrs. Ruth Hill Beacon, Route 1, Hood River, Oregon

d. When an application form is furnished the applicant by the firm, it should be filled out neatly and accurately. The data sheet is the equivalent of the application blank; hence when an application blank is available, the data sheet is not employed.

The Application Follow-up

115a. If you have received an acknowledgment of your letter or have been granted an interview, write a brief letter of thanks for the courtesy extended.

Dear Mr. Royce:

I wish to thank you for your courtesy in acknowledging my letter of application for a position as private secretary.

Since I shall be in Los Angeles within two weeks, I shall call at your personnel office, as you requested, so that you may personally judge my qualifications for the position for which I applied.

Very truly yours

b. In the follow-up, briefly stress the qualifications that fit you for the position. You may restate important facts from a different point of view, or give new facts, illustrative material, or important details not mentioned in the first letter. Samples of work may also be submitted, or new references may be given.

Dear Mr. Royce:

Thank you for your kindness in allowing me, at this morning's interview, to tell you why I feel that I can satisfactorily fill the position of private secretary to you.

From the time I entered high school until the present, all my preparation has centered on this kind of work. While in high school, I began my preparation by taking the secretarial course. At college I majored in secretarial training, receiving several prizes for proficiency in typing and shorthand. My practical experience, as you know, includes several summers' work with firms in Medford and two years with the World Insurance Company of Portland.

I consider my work not merely a job, but a career. Should I be successful, I believe that my training, experience, and interest will assure you a competent, efficient secretary.

Very truly yours,

c. **Make reference to preceding letters tactful to avoid displaying petulance at your failure so far to receive the position. (Some authorities recommend that with the follow-up the writer enclose a carbon copy of the original letter and data sheet on thin copy paper.)**

Dear Mr. Wadhams:

Several weeks ago I applied for a position as playground supervisor for the coming summer. You informed me that there was no vacancy at that time, but that you would place my application on file should any of your present appointees be unable to take up their duties.

May I ask whether there is any vacancy now? If you refer to my letter of application, you will find, I think, that I have the background, training, and experience that you require in the persons you select as supervisors of public playgrounds.

I am so very much interested in this type of work that at Blank College, where I am majoring in Social Service, I have taken all the courses offered in physical education with reference to directing organized group games.

If your staff is now complete, won't you keep me in mind should a vacancy occur?

Very truly yours,

d. **Write the follow-up immediately after receiving an interview or an acknowledgment.**

Index

INDEX

D

INDEX

INDEX

J

K

L

M

INDEX

INDEX